SURFCASTER

The Ultimate Surf Fishing Guide

William A. Muller

Al inquiries should be addressed to:

SURFCASTING LLC

P.O. BOX 10665

Westbury, NY 11590

ISBN 978-1-4507-8266-1

Design and Layout: Stacey Kruk

www.skgraphics.net

Cover Design : Tommy Corrigan

PREFACE

This book is intended as a more or less complete book of surf fishing; at least as it is done on the east coast. It is, therefore, an encyclopedic format. It is also only one person's point of view: mine. There are other views and philosophies and the reader should keep that in mind as we progress through the book.

It is my goal to include lots of help for the guy or gal just getting started, yet offer plenty of information and ideas for the well-seasoned angler too. That may be presumptuous and even overly ambitious, but Zeno agreed to let me give it a try. It is, in some ways, a modern-day version of the wildly successful Surf Fishing With The Experts that was first printed in the mid 1980s. However, in the new millennium so much of that book, although historically interesting, doesn't play today. The nitty-gritty details about equipment and situations are well out of date. For example, few people were seriously discussing graphite rods, braided lines, or high-tech reel designs back then, yet in the modern surf fishing world these are almost necessary apparatus for so many anglers. So, regardless of one's ability and experience level, we hope the information found in this book will accelerate your learning curve as well as increase your respect, appreciation, and enjoyment of surf fishing.

I've always believed, be it through seminars, articles, or books, that the best I can do for you is to share the information, presentations, and ideas that have worked for me.

INTRODUCTION

Any serious discourse about the sport of surf fishing begins with a definition. What is it? A simple definition defines it as standing in the "surf" and casting with lures or bait in an attempt to catch fish. It turns out, however, that this definition falls short because it fails to take into account that the execution of the sport does vary under different conditions, or that it has differing meanings to various people. So, in reality, you will create your own definition as you answer some questions about yourself and the sport that are posed in this book.

Begin with these questions. Who am I, and what do I expect to get out of the sport? Do I want to be a laid back casual angler, or am I seeking an intense competitive experience. Do I prefer to fish only on bluebird days? Can I also relish being tossed about in the surf on the meanest weather days? Do I mainly want to connect with other people or can I enjoy myself by myself? How good do I want to become at the sport? These are some of the questions that will help you with your definition and assist you as you set a course in this new endeavor.

I hope you will never forget that you entered this sport to have fun, regardless of the details of your personal definition. When it isn't fun anymore one of two things must be considered. First, the sport has lost its interest for me, or second, how have I lost my way as I navigated my participation in surf fishing?

I would offer a caution at this stage because I've seen how the attitudes and temptations of the world have evolved in recent decades. Today, everything is hyped. It seems to me, as I watch and listen to a swirl of visual and printed fodder, that nothing is good enough on its own. So, for example, a good movie can't just be good: well-written, well acted, well directed, and enjoyable, it has to be the second coming of D.W. Griffith. Stop there: just go look it up.

How does this pertain to surf fishing? Well, to explain my point let me relate a recent experience. I had a really great afternoon last fall fishing a tide after all the early morning guys had left. I was all alone, halfway between two parking lots, from 1 pm to 4:30 pm. At about 4:30 pm a few guys showed up and fished immediately in front of the parking lot entrances to the sand. No one was within a thousand feet of me. By 4:30 pm, the action had actually begun to quiet down, although we still picked a few fish. The next day I arrived at the same stage of the tide and a guy approached me, almost out of breath, and regaled me with a breathless over-hyped, over-sold story. I heard the same story that day from three different breathless anglers. Of course, since I was fishing off by myself the day before, neither of the men knew I was actually there, and so believed they were providing me with important fishing information. Here's what they said.

1. You should have been here yesterday.
2. I caught many, many keepers into the mid-twenties.
3. Everyone had thirty or forty fish.
4. I caught them right here where we're standing.

Okay, here's my translation.

1. I was there yesterday.
2. The biggest fish caught was my sixteen-pound fish.
3. I caught twenty-two fish and it took three hours, others arrived too late and didn't have enough time to catch that many.
4. I was the only one standing in the spot they described.

If reality isn't good enough for you, I suggest you find something else to do. Some other hobby to excite you. The reason? Reality will never live up to hype, so embrace the reality and value it. That also holds true when you read fishing reports or listen to buddies. Dial it back and you'll have a better picture. Instead of thrusting yourself in the middle of a perceived and hyped-up fishing experience, think about how you can improve your skills and perhaps you will be able to lead the day. I know that when I'm having a difficult time I'm not so proud that I can't take advice from anyone who has the "edge" that day. Still, I encounter many surf rats with mediocre skills that refuse my help, seem to prefer the hype, and are comfortable with at least a partially invented experience. I vaguely remember a fantasy called *Alice In Wonderland*. Although I enjoy the fantasy of a book or movie, I prefer real life to be real and it's plenty good enough for me.

As long as we're talking about hyperbole, let's talk about another manifestation of it: namely, the "big striper" fixation. Avoid the "big bass" hype that creates a big fish snob who is unable to enjoy an everyday surf angling experience. A big fish snob gradually becomes blinded to the variety of enjoyable aspects of surf fishing. To my way of thinking, I should be able to enjoy a two-pound bass as well as a forty-pound striper. They aren't the same, but they are all fun to find, trick, and catch. Fast fishing for small stripers has taught me a lot about the personalities and temperament of their larger cousins, and I've applied this knowledge toward better personal success. Don't stick your nose up at bluefish either. They aren't nearly as easy to catch as most people say they are. Yes, in an all-out blitz they are easy to catch, but so are stripers. In my experience, the hardest fish to catch consistently is weakfish, and even this species offers us days when they feed with abandon: just fewer tides than stripers and blues.

Finally comes the question of how to use this book. We hope there's something in here for everyone, but most anglers will be served best if they begin at chapter one and gradually move through the book. The nice thing about a book, not shared by videos, is the ability to conveniently read a sentence again and again, savor it, until understanding has been achieved. It is impossible to convey all the nuances of techniques no matter how hard I might try, but I suspect nuggets of information are hidden in the sentences, nonetheless, and perhaps I don't even know they are there. That's why savoring and not rushing is the best approach.

The book is arranged so that the first two chapters guide the reader into the sport from the beginning. That is, from the moment someone begins to think about giving surf fishing a try. If you're well beyond that point, you may want to skip to chapter three or read the first two chapters just for amusement.

Please read the *conservation ethic* material as well as the *catch and release* sections because although surf fishing is a blood sport, true sportsmen come to the sport with additional understandings, philosophies, and appreciations. One of these is the desire to be able to catch fish year after year and become part of an effort to prevent humans from over harvesting. Remember, it was sportsmen who were responsible for the conservation ethic in the United States that began at the turn of the 20th century. President Teddy Roosevelt was an occasional fisherman and avid hunter and was the first to establish wildlife preserves which this country continues to enjoy today. Further, it was Trout Unlimited that saved trout streams and conserved trout. It was Ducks Unlimited that did the same for waterfowl and it was organizations such as Save Our Stripers that awakened a debate about striped bass stocks that ultimately led to a better management approach. This is as much a part of our heritage as is the harvesting of our living resources, and it must be nurtured forever or someday we will lose this sport.

TABLE OF CONTENTS

Chapter 7

Chapter 8

Chapter 9

Chapter 10

Chapter 11

Chapter 12

Chapter 1
A PARTIAL HISTORY OF SURF FISHING

A Little History Of Modern Surf Fishing:

Many, if not most, of the founders of the modern sport were veterans of World War II. For those anglers who were born in the last quarter of the 20th century it may be difficult to understand how quickly surf fishing evolved after WW II. In fact, the history of surf fishing has taken many interesting turns in the last two centuries. At one time in the 1800s surf fishing was the domain of the wealthy and was done mostly from a type of high, often-rickety, pier called a "stand." Striped bass were the fish they primarily tried to catch and so these high piers were often just called "bass stands." Stands were popular along the New England coast for decades.

In the early days, wealthy landed gentry were the main builders and users of the stands. Basically, a "bass stand" was a high lane of wood planking supported on wood "pins" or posts derived from local trees such as oaks, and secured between and into boulders. Obviously, this type of construction limited the number of locations where stands could be built. Furthermore, the form of construction made them vulnerable to storms: especially hurricanes and severe nor'easters. Wealthy gentlemen had their servants collect lobsters and trash fish. It has been frequently reported that on Sunday morning these wealthy men would go to church in their finest attire, including high hats that were popular in that century, and after church proceed to the "stand."

While the gentry were at church, the workers chopped up the fish and lobsters (yes, they were that abundant back in the 1800s) and chum with them from the top of the stand. Lobster tails were reserved for bait. When the wealthy men arrived at the stands, striped bass were happily feeding on the lobster and fish chunks around the stand. Striped bass were also more

Cuttyhunk, MA

abundant then, and so it wasn't difficult for these men to catch many striped bass. Their sport was sanitized because workers, often referred to as Islanders in New England spots such as Cuttyhunk, did the dirty work of chumming and handling fish. Thus, many reports and drawings described the gentlemen as fishing in the same Sunday finery they wore to church. How much of the information provided in these disparate sources is apocryphal and how much is accurate is difficult to ascertain.

Although details of stand fishing changed in the 20th Century as the social structure on the New England coast changed, it's clear that the practice continued in some form well into the 20th Century. It seemed that at some point the landed gentry formed clubs to facilitate their hobby. In time, as the 20th Century progressed and many of the wealthy men took up other newly introduced hobbies such as tennis and golf, maintenance of the stands was taken over by less wealthy men and in time the middle class dominated the clubs. The conversion of surf fishing from a wealthy man's hobby to a sport for everyone occurred gradually as society changed, and clearly society underwent a severe metamorphosis in the first half of the 20th Century. Gradually, the once common practice of fishing for striped bass from stands faded as more and more stands were destroyed in storms or rotted away, and clubs lacked the financial resources to rebuild them. It is also true that anglers in clubs discovered the joys of fishing from the sand. But, there were other social changes on the horizon that would not only alter the face of surf fishing, but change America too.

Average citizens in the first half of the 20th Century typically received low pay, and worked six days a week with long hours. Therefore, few people had either the time or the money for surf fishing. Most workers who enjoyed fishing did so from party boats that were much more numerous at the time in comparison to the size of the coastal population. Many anglers became "regulars" and hopped onto their favorite boat every Saturday or Sunday toting a burlap sack at their side. I saw snippets of this when I was a boy. In the 1950s, my father took me flounder fishing on party boats out of Captree. We typically made a number of trips in April and May, and I would notice many of the same men every time we went. I also noted that each man had a favorite spot at the rail, and could be found at the same place each trip. This was the way it was, but things were soon to change.

The influence of unions grew rapidly throughout the early part of the century. The result was better wages, a shorter workweek, and a shorter working day. Then there was the G.I. Bill of Rights and many returning W.W. II veterans took advantage of it by going to college and earning degrees that were their tickets to professional jobs, higher salaries, better benefits, and more leisure time. The country also enjoyed prosperity in the 1950s that raised the average pay of workers. It was also a period of incredible expansion of the suburb concept. To provide a perspective, Brooklyn was once the suburb of New York City (Manhattan) in the 1800s. This was seen as an advantage; in no small part due to the fact people could get on a subway and be at work in minutes. However, with more money, more technology, more leisure time, and affordable automobiles, workers wanted to live closer to the places where they recreated and not where they worked. Entrepreneurs soon took advantage of these desires and vast tracks of small affordable easy to build homes began to pop up, such as Levittown in Long Island's Nassau County. People moved to these "new" suburbs in droves.

Limited Lure Selection:

It should also be noted that anglers plying the beaches in the first half of the 20th Century had a very limited number of lures to pick from. There were bucktails (not as sophisticated as today's models). There were also lead-head feather jigs that were more often trolled than cast, and there were metal lures too, but I rarely saw them chromed like today's tins are. Instead they were cast from tin or an alloy of tin and lead, but left unfinished. My father and uncle sometimes took me to Jones Beach, and one of my boyhood jobs was to rub these metal lures in the sand to remove any oxidation and induce a shine.

There were also quite a few large freshwater plugs on the market intended for muskies and northern pike, but they usually weren't through-wired and they were of questionable durability. Some anglers adapted these to saltwater use by changing the hardware, while others took up the challenge of turning homemade designs on small lathes. Painting was another challenge. Eventually, inspired beach rats developed the practice of soaking wood plugs in linseed oil and letting them dry, before painting them and adding hardware. Despite a limited arsenal, early surf fishermen honed their skills to a sharp edge and sculptured the modern style of surf fishing into a form they relished and one we continue to follow. Frank Woolner, late friend and big-wig of *The Saltwater Sportsman*, was fond of saying that the best surf fishermen in the world were found in places with just enough fish to make things interesting, but not so many fish as to encourage anglers to become lazy and sloppy. Frank was a firm believer in the concept of trial by fire.

Mid Century Technology:

Here comes the technology express. Not only did technology bring us fantastic new cars, appliances, health care wonders such as penicillin, and cheap suburban homes, but also new materials and designs. More and more spinning reels made their way to the United States from France in the 1950s, and plastics were adapted to more and more uses that made many products affordable. Chemistry produced the marvels of DDT (yes, once considered a miracle and safe bug killer) and also new types of resins. It wasn't long before these resins were used to make fiberglass boats and rods. Take it from me; wood boats are a drag to maintain. I know, because it was my job to scrape, caulk, and paint the family boat every spring. Sure, there is maintenance on fiberglass boats too, but there's just no comparison to what's required for wood boats.

At about the same time, monofilament lines replaced linen lines. For those of you who are unfamiliar with linen lines, they were natural fiber lines that rotted and frayed so easily that they became worthless in weeks if used in saltwater and not washed and dried. It was my job to wash the lines and weave them across the backyard lawn to dry. Are you beginning to get the idea that surf fishing back in the day wasn't just a "day at the beach?"

The point is that it became a lot easier to become a fisherman in the 1950s, and many did enter the sport in the decade. The number of beach fishermen expanded too. Some decided to use WW II surplus four-wheel drive jeeps on the beaches to get around. Later, some of these anglers adapted VWs to the beach, finding the lightweight of the "beetle" combined with large balloon tires a perfect match for the sand. They also redefined the sport of surf fishing and it is their concept that many of us still use today. There was no manual or rule book, but these WW II vets invented the rules and by-laws and passed them down to newcomers, one by one by mouth, until a vast army of beach anglers plied the surf from north of Massachusetts to the Carolinas.

Competitive Surf Fishing:

The Schaefer Brewing Company sponsored a coast-wide fishing tournament for many years in the mid 20th Century. This sponsorship stimulated interest in surf fishing and, since only clubs could join, the number of surf fishing clubs increased

(Zeno Hromin photo)

sharply. Eventually, the financial burden of sponsorship weighed too heavily on Schaefer and the company was forced to end the affiliation.

After less than a decade later, a small cadre of Long Island Clubs decided to invent a new surf-fishing contest based upon the Schaefer Contest. Representatives from these clubs managed to put together a set of rules to govern the contest and the New York Surf Fishing Contest was launched in 1980. Within a short time, *The Long Island Fisherman* assumed sponsorship of the season-long contest and as of this writing continues their support. The popularity of the contest grew quickly and within a few years was well subscribed. In these decades, representation typically involved 15 to 19 clubs and five hundred to almost 1000 anglers. The contest has acquired quite a bit of prestige over the years, so much so that even non-surf anglers keep track of the contest.

The New Millennium:

If we look back on the last hundred years of surf fishing and then describe the sport today, one could easily be awed by the comparison. The stands are gone, the era of the wealthy aristocratic angler is gone. The suburbs are glutted with regular middle class "Joes" who enjoy fishing. We have fancy high-tech four-wheel drive vehicles instead of war-surplus jeeps. Most of us fish with braided lines that provide us with many advantages over monofilament. We have graphite and composite material rods that are so far removed from the early fiberglass tools that it becomes difficult to attempt a comparison. We have a vast array of lures; many of which are impossible to make without modern technology. And, last but not least, we have hi-tech reels made of space-age materials and engineered with incredible precision. These reels are more powerful, endure saltwater better, and are much more reliable than the tools I first used decades ago. I often ask myself how I fished without modern reels, braided line, and graphite rods. I guess my point is that newcomers to the sport have a vast array of advantages over those who honed their craft in post WW II America. Therefore, it seems to me, that all of us have a responsibility to stay the course on an up-sloped learning curve as well as maintain a commitment to understand the sport invented a half-century ago by imaginative and resourceful anglers. So many of these pioneers also led the fight to protect our living marine resources that perhaps they deserve to be honored by us as we also commit to a powerful conservation ethic.

Today's surf fishermen have hi-tech sophisticated beach vehicles to assist us. (Zeno Hromin photo)

Chapter 2
THE FIRST YEAR

So, perhaps you have a buddy who has tried to get you to go surf fishing with him. Maybe it was a relative who took you when you were young and now you want to get back to it. Maybe you watched people on the beaches last fall, saw them catch fish, and thought "this is pretty good stuff, and I want to know more." Whatever your motivation, you need to get started, and that's what this chapter is all about. As your guide on the "yellow brick road" I feel compelled to begin with one very important idea. **Don't commit to the sport financially until you've had some time to figure out whether you hate it, like it, or love it.** Give yourself a season to figure this out before you spend a ton of money. That said, you will have to spend a little money unless you have someone willing to lend equipment to you.

How Much and for What:

Prices go up, and sometimes come down. They are influenced by inflation and deflation, and finally outlets run sales for some products and not for others. The point is that the prices that follow are intended only as a guide, and should be viewed in the

This gaggle of anglers sport rods and reels from low-end to hi-end. (Zeno Hromin photo)

light of your present salary, the state of the economy, and the value of the dollar. As the years pass, the actual dollar values will change but not so much if viewed as a percentage of your income.

Keep the gear simple for the first year. Don't worry about accessories that may become essentials in a year or two. The first year you can get by with a rod and reel, line, waders, a waterproof jacket (top) and a few lures.

Rod:

Begin with a spinning rod and reel. Although it is possible to spend $1000 for a rod, don't go there yet. If you shop around you'll find a serviceable quality rod for about $100, give or take $20. The exact price will depend upon the length you choose, the model you select, and the level of quality. If you shop around and look for a sale, you'll find a good rod in this range. Actually, I suggest you choose a one-piece nine-foot medium power rod at the start because it should serve you well in almost all surf fishing venues. I can tell you that most of the time I use my nine-foot Lamiglass GSB 1M and it serves me well. I perused a few 2011 catalogs and found several good rods from brand

Custom rod builders create top-quality rods to fit an angler's fishing style. (Zeno Hromin photo)

name manufacturers costing under $100. Advances in technology have simplified the process of making a graphite rod and that saves us money. The process of automated rod wrapping has improved and lowered the cost too, and the prices of some raw materials has declined. The result is massed-produced quality rods at reasonable prices. Although I urge you to avoid spending large sums the first year, let me also caution you to avoid the $69 "combo special." It may be difficult for the novice to appreciate the tremendous difference between the cheap combo and an inexpensive serviceable rod, but trust me there is a huge difference. One final caution: whatever rod you decide on, make sure it is **one-piece!** Regardless of how small your vehicle is, or how limited your storage space is, do not buy a two-piece rod. This is another situation where you'll just have to trust me. Two years from now you'll understand clearly.

Reel:

Again I caution you to avoid the very cheapest reels because they will not provide the essential qualities needed to deal with casting and retrieving, fighting fish, the corrosive nature of saltwater, and a need for reliability. A quality spinning reel is much more important than the rod so, if you have to choose, put your money in the reel. That said, I looked over available saltwater reels and found more than a half-dozen reels that will work for you and cost between $80 and $120. Remember, the rod and reel selected only has to last one year. In reality, the tackle may last several years, but if you get involved in the sport you'll want to make a move up in quality. The outfit you first select can become your backup when you upgrade your equipment.

The size of the reel is crucial. Let's assume you take my advice and select a nine-foot rod. One of the worst things you can do is match the rod with either a reel that's too big or too small. Too small and the reel will lack power, casting distance will be reduced, and the outfit will be out of balance. Too large and the outfit will be out of balance and the loops of line that spill off the spool will be too wide for the guides. The result will be shorter casts and a tendency for the line to bunch together and form knots.

A balanced outfit is very important. A balanced rod and reel should create a balancing point on the fore-grip in front of the reel. When an outfit is out of balance it negatively affects casting distance, casting accuracy, and enhances angler fatigue. So, how does one select the correct reel size for the nine-foot rod? There a two ways to go about this.

One approach is to use the reel's model number as a guide. So, for the nine-foot rod, look at reels numbered as 55-65, 550-650, or 5500-6500. Those are medium size reels and most will do the job. Not all manufacturers conform their model numbers to this number system, but many do. Also, avoid narrow spool designs because they don't work well in saltwater situations. Don't panic if your selected size is a little off, because it's just an estimate. Put the reel on the rod and if it looks odd, go one step up or down in size and see if the balance point is on the fore-grip, and it simply looks "right."

A second way of estimating the right size for the reel is to look at how much it weighs. Reels that weigh between 16-20 ounces are appropriate for the nine-foot rod as long as they boast wide spools. Once again, the ultimate test is to try and balance the outfit on your finger somewhere on the fore-grip. If it balances, then the combo will work.

Line:

Advising you about line is one of the trickiest jobs I have in this book. The reason is the enormous differences between monofilament and braided lines. Mono is cheaper and easier to work with, but is much less sensitive, stretches a lot, and breaks down faster than braid. Generally, beginners do better with monofilament because it is easier to use. However, the advantages of braid are overwhelming, and most of you will use it someday anyway, so you might want to try it right off the bat. Braid is more expensive, more durable, has lasting knot strength, doesn't stretch, provides more sensitivity, and has better hook setting ability. A 650-yard spool of 20 pound-test monofilament line; such as Trilene Big Game line, will cost about $10. That's enough line to fill your reel's spool two or three times. A 125-

Monofilament line, simple leaders, and an improved clinch knot is a logical approach to line in the first year. (Zeno Hromin photo)

yard spool of 20 pound-test braid; such as Stren Sonic Braid, will cost $15 dollars and will only allow you to half-fill the typical reel spool once. The first half of the reel's spool is filled with 20 pound-test monofilament line called "the backing."

Regardless of the line you choose, I suggest you have an experienced angler, or an employee from a tackle shop wind the line on the reel, so it is done correctly to avoid twist. If you select braided line, have that experienced person tie the correct connecting knot between the "backing" and the braid. Set the reel's drag at about 1/3 of the pound test of the running line, or about 5-7 pounds of pull. Beware, that's a lot of pulling power, but more about that later.

A Few Things About Braid:

Braid is actually easy to use if you are reasonably coordinated and observe a few cautions. First, you have to pay more attention to braid than monofilament line. That means we must look at the spool before we cast, and look at the spool after the cast to make sure there are no loops of line sticking up from the tight coils of line on the spool. Loose loops end up becoming "wind knots" if left unattended, and these knots are almost impossible to take out of braid. If you spot a loop, peel off line by hand while walking backward until the loop comes off the spool and straightens. Then, wind the line back on the reel with a little tension applied with two fingers on the line ahead of the spool. If all this seems to be a bit much for you at this stage, then fill the spool from bottom to top with the 20 pound-test monofilament line.

Leaders:

You'll need a few thirty-pound test leaders. Don't fuss over this. Buy a package (5-6 leaders) at your local bait and tackle dealer. It's cheap (a few dollars) and avoids the problem of knot tying. If you buy pre-made leaders, you'll have a reliable product and all you'll need to do is learn to tie one *simple* knot to connect the leader to the main line, also called the running line. Tie the main line to the leader on the swivel end of the leader.

The Knot:

One of easiest fishing knots to tie is the improved clinch knot. If tied correctly it will have a breaking strength of about 95% of the pound-test of the line. I'll not take space to describe it here because you can find diagrams and descriptions online, in books, and handout sheets in stores. However, let me emphasize these points. One, use 6 turns if you use monofilament line, and 9-10 turns if you use braid. Second, always moisten the line with saliva before pulling the knot tight. Third, always pull on the tag line to remove slack. Fourth, always examine the knot carefully and reject it if you see bulges or loops in the knot. Once the knot is pulled tight it should look like a stack of coins. If it doesn't, cut it and tie it again. Poorly tied knots are the cause of 95% of all disconnects with lures and fish. Tie a good knot and be confident.

Waders:

You can pay hundreds of dollars for a pair of waders, but you don't have too. My everyday waders cost $70 dollars. I get a

This angler is dressed appropriately: waders, top over waders, snug utility belt with safety pliers. (Zeno Hromin photo)

year, and sometimes a year and a half out of them before they fall apart, but I have to tell you I didn't get longer life out of the two and three hundred dollar models I've tried. I buy Cabela's Three Forks 420 Denier Featherweight lug sole waders. I can't imagine finding a better or more cost-efficient set of waders.

Top:

This is optional. If you don't plan to fish in rough water, stand deep in the water, or fish on rainy days, you can skip this accessory. However, if you do intend to plunge into the breach of surf fishing you'll need a pullover top for safety reasons. The pullover waterproof garment goes over the waders and is tied tight to the waist with a belt or length of rope. If you fall, this arrangement buys some time, giving you a chance to get up and out of the water before your waders fill up. Once the waders fill, your chances of standing up and getting out of the rough water are slim to none! Tie the top securely. A decent top costs about $100.

Lures:

Bombers are examples of reliable, affordable and productive lures. (Ross Squire photo)

Don't go crazy the first year. Keep it simple and don't fall for the idea that one must have a particular model or color. The "I must have it" way of looking at things is bogus 95% of the time, and until you are well immersed in the sport, don't compile a huge arsenal of lures. Here's what's in my bag and it's all you need for now. Start with several 2 to 2 ½ -ounce pencil poppers (Tactical Angler's SeaPencil, or Gibbs Pencil Popper). The cost will be about $20. Select two standard poppers of the same weight (Super Strike Little Neck Poppers). The cost will be about $20. Add two A-Salt Bombers if you intend to try night fishing. The cost will be about $15. Now you'll need two metal lures (tins) in 1½ to 2-ounce sizes. I prefer the West End Tackle Charlie Graves styles. The cost will be about $12-15 depending on the size of the lures. Finally, add one 1-ounce and one 1¼-ounce Uncle Josh white bucktail along with a jar of Uncle Josh red and white porkrind (model 240-S). The cost will be about $15. The total cost for the lures will be about $85.

Total Cost:

The estimate of total cost to get started is based on the following. I used an average price for the rod and reel, excluded the top, and averaged the possible prices for lures, leaders, and line. The estimate assumes you'll use a rope belt or old pant belt for the first year. Obviously buying items on sale, borrowing items from others, and picking up a few things at garage sales could cut this total significantly. Before you freak out, think about what it would cost to begin bowling, tennis, or any other hobby. Be creative and keep the cost down the first year. Good luck getting into a great sport!

Summary:

Rod:	$100
Reel:	$80
Waders:	$70
Line:	$15
Leaders:	$5
Lures:	$ 85
Total:	$385

Chapter 3
THE SECOND YEAR

Well?

Great! You survived your first year in surf fishing. Well, what do you think? Was it great? Was it okay? Was it a waste of your time? If you answered "yes" to either question 2 or 3, then you don't need me anymore. If you answered "yes" to question 1, then read on. To actually have a meaningful answer you should have gone surf fishing at least 20 times in the previous year. Let's assume you invested the time, and we'll shuffle right along to making a move up in grade and style.

No Intermediates:

This is my opinion and others may differ with me, but just as I don't believe in making a large investment in the sport until you find out you really like it, so too I don't believe in upgrading incrementally. If you really like the sport, you'll go often, and if you go often you'll start learning fast. If you really like the sport, you won't be content with a flat or slow learning curve. You'll start reading a lot about the sport, you'll ask questions of other surf rats, and you'll start attending surf fishing seminars and asking questions too. It is likely, therefore, that your knowledge and ability will blossom. If that happens, you'll surpass the value of your original tackle in short order. So, since you already know you love the sport, why not start the process of reaching for top quality tackle now.

Stick to the Nine-Foot Outfit:

Let's stay with the model of a nine-foot medium power tackle outfit introduced in chapter one. That way, we have the convenience and ease of relating the information in one chapter with that in another. However, "we're moving on up." Perhaps you remember the television show *The Jeffersons* that was popular a few decades back. The theme song had those words and indeed if you're ready, let's move up.

Rod:

My nine-foot graphite outfit is a Lamiglas blank (model GSB 108-1M). The rod was made by a local professional with components that have proven to allow for long casts, powerful hook sets and fighting ability, and yet can cast anything from one-half ounce to almost four ounces. If you are going to invest in a quality rod blank, then I advise you to consult a professional rod builder and have the rod made up correctly. This rod does almost everything that my eleven-foot Lamiglas (model GSB 132-1M) can do. If you can own only one rod, this is the way to go. If you don't like this particular blank, consult with your rod builder about other choices. The keys here are to use a quality blank, use quality components, and stick to a medium power rod with a medium action tip. Blanks rated as "light" will not be able to cast heavier lures, will not have the catapulting force to make strong casts into a wind, and provides less hook setting ability. A blank rated "heavy" will be too stiff to cast smaller lighter lures and will produce shorter casts. "Fast" tip action rods may produce a bigger bend when fighting schoolies, but it isn't the correct tip action for casting heavy lures and fighting heavy fish. A "slow" tip action limits the ability to cast small lighter lures. Moderate or medium tip action is the workhorse for most situations in the surf. A top quality one-piece medium power nine-foot surf rod will cost between $200 and $400 depending on the specific blank and the components you choose. You'll regret it if you turn this blank into a two-piece rod. Yet another thing you'll just have to trust me about. Let me put it another way. I don't know any committed experienced surf anglers who use two-piece rods.

Reel:

I said in chapter one that the reel is more important than the rod. I meant it. There are some good reels out there for approximately $400, but they lack enough power, reliability, and length of life for my liking. They'll work okay, but you'll replace

A properly filled spool maximizes casting distance and minimizes "wind" knots. (Zeno Hromin photo)

them more frequently and you'll feel as if they are just a little short of the mark.

So, don't fool around, go to the top, and have a reel for the rest of your life if you maintain it. I match a Van Staal 200 to my nine-foot Lamiglas. The reel will set you back about $740, but it's more than worth it in my opinion. As a member of the Van Staal Pro Team, I've owned several of these reels for decades. That's right, decades! With proper maintenance the reels will last a lifetime.

How Reliable?

Just how durable and reliable are top quality reels like the Van Staal brand? In order to answer this question, I dug into my logs for the last twenty years and extracted the following information. Before I give you the numbers, let me set the parameters.

My Experience:

Two nine-foot one-piece Lamiglass 1M rods
Two VS 200 reels
Braided line (20-pound test)
Twenty years elapsed time
Many thousands of fish caught

Here's the bottom line after making a few calculations from information in my log. In twenty years each reel was used for about 4410 hours and caught approximately 20,000 fish. The fish ranged from small to very large and included stripers, weakfish, and bluefish. So now you understand why I say that when I use this equipment I don't worry about the reel. Van Staal reels have a solid track record, I trust them, and because they haven't failed me in key moments, I am therefore able to focus on my presentations and on analyzing the behavior of bait and gamefish.

Alternative: Conventional Tackle:

In my opinion, spinning rods and reels have evolved to a level of high performance so that conventional tackle is no longer necessary. That said; there is still a cadre of anglers who enjoy and prefer conventional tackle, especially for bait fishing. Conventional tackle consists of a revolving spool reel (similar to a freshwater bait casting reel) and a rod with a series of smaller eyed guides. The rods used are generally a little more powerful. That is, they are often a tad stiffer (especially when used for bait fishing) and can easily handle heavier lures and sinkers. Decades ago, spinning rods were made of fiberglass and not graphite, they tended to be whippy, and they didn't load as well as today's spinning rods. Therefore, we used conventional rods when we needed more power or while fishing in the ocean with bait and heavy sinkers. Many anglers claim that revolving spool reels give them a better feel when a fish picks up the bait, and that it is easier to adjust to the movements of the fish prior to setting the hook. I don't disagree with this point, and now that you have committed to the sport you may want to do some reading about conventional tackle as well as questioning experts on the subject at fishing shows and seminars. With knowledge about conventional gear you'll be in a better position to decide whether you want to add this gear to your arsenal.

Line:

If you decided to work with braid the first season, stick with it. If you used monofilament last season, it's time to move to braid. Braid simply offers an angler too many advantages to be relegated to a corner or not used at all. I am confident that any and all problems a person may have with braid can be corrected with a little bit of effort. A brief review is in order. With the nine-foot outfit I use twenty-pound test braided line, and thirty-pound test with my eleven-foot outfit. I prefer either Sufix

Performance Braid or Stren Sonic Braid.

Second year anglers might want to upgrade the quality of their tackle. (Zeno Hromin photo)

A good time to attempt to deal with some typical angler complaints about braid is the second season because by that time an angler has acquired enough basic casting skills and understanding to be able to correct poor casting habits. In short, an angler can be sloppy with monofilament line and get away with it, but sloppy won't work with braid. Another axiom to keep in mind is the truth that I accepted long ago and you'll need to accept sooner rather than later. Namely, anglers are the cause of 99.99% of the problems they have with tackle. As long as the equipment is of good quality, we're the cause of our problems. Consider break-offs, for example. Almost all break-offs are the result of badly tied knots and not the line, the reel, or the rod.

So, here's a list of cautions about braided line.

1. **Do not overfill the reel spool.** With mono the rule of thumb is to spool to within 1/8-inch of the lip of the spool. For braid, leave ¼-inch of space.
2. **Pay attention to your casts:** Anticipate the moment when the lure hits the water and stop the line loops from leaving the spool as the lure lands in the water. Do not let loops of

line continue to cascade off the spool after the lure is in the water. These "extra" loops will create overlays, spool loops, and under-cutting when you begin the retrieve. These anomalies on the spool turn into wind knots and "birds nests" during the cast.

3. **Check your reel as you retrieve.** A quick glance will suffice to tell you if the line is wrapped around the drag nut or if there are any reel anomalies. If you notice this, stop the retrieve, open the bail or take the line off the roller, and begin stripping off line by hand. Walk backwards as you do this because a pile of line on the sand will turn into knots and birds nests too. When you reach the anomaly you can begin reeling in the loose line. Use your thumb and index finger on the line to create mild pressure so that the line goes on the spool easily. Remember, there is no water pressure on the loose line to assist in laying the line nicely on the spool.
4. **Stick with a simple knot:** Use the improved clinch knot because it is so easy to tie and when tied correctly, has 95% of the strength of the line used to tie it. There are lots of good uses for other modern knots and I'm not suggesting you shouldn't use them. Rather, for the first few seasons keep the process as simple as possible. Remember to make nine or ten turns with the braided line in order for this knot to be tied correctly and not break or slip.

Monofilament Line:

If you are uncomfortable using braided line don't fret. There are quality monofilament lines on the market and, although braid offers advantages over monofilament, mono remains a solid line choice. Avoid inexpensive brands for two reasons. First, monofilament is not expensive, so why put up with cut-rate brands. Second, good monofilament lines are manufactured with specific qualities that help the angler, such as knot strength and abrasion resistance. Use fifteen-pound test mono on a nine-foot tackle combo and twenty-pound test on an eleven-foot outfit. Many anglers trust Big Game line, and I used it exclusively before braided line came along.

Fluorocarbon Line:

My first comment about using fluorocarbon line in temperate saltwater fishing is: SAVE YOUR MONEY! Fluorocarbon is a relatively expensive line that has its place in the angling world, but doesn't serve any real purpose in our plankton-rich, turbid North Atlantic waters. Even on the calmest days with the cleanest water, there is still a lot of plankton and suspended fine particles in the water and it isn't clear at all. There is no advantage to using fluorocarbon line when fishing from the Mid-Atlantic to the northern tip of Maine. However, if you make regular winter trips to Florida or the Bahamas, well then please bring that fluorocarbon. Tropical and sub-tropical waters contain much less suspended matter and far less plankton, the fish all have gigantic eyes for their size, and fluorocarbon is a huge advantage, but not here.

A quality surf bag provides secure storage and easy access to the lures inside. (Zeno Hromin photo)

Surf Bag:

I didn't suggest a surf bag for the first year in order to keep costs down, but the second year you'll need to think about buying one. I strongly urge you to purchase a smaller rather than a larger bag. The largest surf bags may hold more, but they fatigue our necks and shoulders quickly and my experience has taught me that you'll never use all the lures in one outing. The second year is a good time for us to rid ourselves of our fears (using braided line, for example). Here's another fear to get over. It is futile to try and carry enough lures to cover every possible scenario, so don't try. Yes, color can be important, but most of the time it's useless to worry about it because it doesn't matter. Just remember, white is right! Almost everything that stripers and blues eat has a white belly and most have silver and white sides. White is not an alien color to gamefish. I use white bucktails 90% of the time and with great success, and when friends tell me I need a Bomber, bottle plug, or darter of a certain color I just ignore them. I fish whatever colors I've tucked into my bag and catch fish. Furthermore, I tutor promising newcomers from time to time, and after a year or two under my wing, I surprise them with a new imposed rule.

Surf belts serve many functions: safety (snug over the top), access to pliers and even a Boga Grip landing tool. (Zeno Hromin photo)

Since, in many cases those I mentor express anxiety about color, I impose a rule either in their second or third year. The rule is they can only use white lures. Immediately they complain, "but I don't have white Bombers, poppers, darters, or bottle plugs." My answer is simple: buy a can of white spray paint. It takes only a month or two for these burgeoning anglers to get over their anxiety about color. At that point the lure count in their surf bags declines sharply. Keep it simple and keep it on target!

Let's get back to a discussion about surf bags. Buy a quality surf bag. I use the smallest bag Van Staal makes. It has four tubes, some slots for tins, and I add a freestanding row of one-inch PVC tubes for bucktails that fits easily in front of the plug tubes. I put one and sometimes two small plugs in each tube. That keeps the weight down. The Van Staal bags are currently being redesigned and should be available at the end of the summer 2011. There are, however, lots of very well made and serviceable lure bags on the market. Some are as big as suitcases, while others are more conservative. To me, less is more.

Total Estimated Cost for New Rod, Reel, & Bag: Approximately $1000

Accessories:

The essential equipment has been discussed previously, but it's time to note that an angler can go nuts when it comes to accessories. There are so many items available that I don't know where to start. So, rather than try to include every little tool and piece of gear, let me reduce the universe to a list of the most-used items.

1. Nine-inch stainless steel needle nose pliers for unhooking fish. A sheath that slips on the waist belt and holds the pliers. Convenience and safety item.
2. Heavy-duty Manley's blunt nose pliers with cutter to easily cut through 3/0 and 4/0 treble hooks. A sheath that slips on the waist belt to hold the pliers. A safety item.
3. Gloves: There are summer weight and cold weather gloves. I wear gloves for safety, warmth, and to get a good grip in cooler weather, and for grip and safety in warm weather. You can pay as little as $2-4 for light woven cotton gloves with gripper dots, or $20 plus for cool weather and "fashion statement" gloves. Less is more.

4. 3.5 mm neoprene waders for cold weather.
5. Hardware for waist belt:
    a. Brass clips attached to the bottom of the surf bag that clip onto "D" rings on the belt. Takes the weight of the bag off your neck and shoulders and puts it onto the hips.
    b. Carabiners on plates on the waist belt to hold telephone cord attachments to pliers.
    c. Lightweight and heavyweight sweatshirts.
    d. Neck light for night fishing only.
    e. SPF 45 U.V. blocker
    f. Baseball style cap.
    g. Wool socks for waders.
    h. Over the head fine-mesh hood for bug control.
    i. Polarized sunglasses.
    j. Neoprene top for cold weather

Total Cost for Significant Accessories: ~ $900-1000
Year Two Equipment Cost: Approximately $2000

Summary of Rod and Reel Outfits

Rod Length	Reel Size	Line lb Test	Usage	Rod Power Graphite
11 feet	VS 300, 275 Others: 600/6000	30-40 lb Braid	Ocean Beaches Fast Water Inlets Heavy Water Heavy Lures	M
9 feet	VS 200 Others: 500/5000	20 lb Braid	Calm Water Lighter Lures	M
7 feet	VS 150	15-20 lb Braid	Small Fish Very Light Lures	M

Power Values For Jetties: MH, H, depending upon angling style.

You'll notice that I recommend "odd" length rods for general use fishing. The reason is that generally, whatever an angler can do with a 10-foot rod, the angler can do with the appropriate 9-foot rod, and likewise a seven-foot rod for an eight-foot rod. If the length is shorter, we save weight and achieve an outfit that is more appropriately balanced. Even lengths, in my opinion, are **niche** sizes: that is, they work best in specific situations. For example, 10-foot medium-heavy and heavy power rods are popular among jetty anglers. They prefer the heavy power so that they can swing fish up to their perch on the rocks, and the shorter length has certain advantages in delivering live eels, working the lure or bait, and managing the final portion of the retrieve up to the rocks.

Summary:

1. The second year is the year to make a move up in quality.
2. Don't move up to intermediate cast tackle. It isn't worth it.
3. The cost to move up will range from approximately $1000 to $2000.
4. Don't think that by buying every nick-knack gadget that they'll improve your angling. They won't, but they will cost money.
5. I use one-piece Lamiglas GSB nine and eleven foot rods equipped with Van Staal reels (200 and 275).

Chapter 4
BEACH VENUES

Big Surf:

There are a variety of surf fishing venues along the striper coast. Some anglers prefer to fish only one type of setting, some fish at a few, while others exploit all venues. Some feature calm water while others, such as ocean beaches and the mouths of inlets, offer heavy surf conditions at times. Waves along ocean beaches can be eight, ten, or more feet high and big waves are difficult to negotiate, but making the effort often pays dividends. Some of the best fishing occurs along ocean beaches when water conditions are tough to deal with, and I urge anglers to be careful in big surf. These "heavy surf" conditions offer real challenges to angler safety as well as problems related to lure presentation. Remember, weather conditions vary and there are plenty of calm ocean days, but fewer in the fall when some of the most important fishing occurs. Many anglers look

Heavy surf conditions offer real challenges to an angler's safety as well as issues of lure presentation. (Zeno Hromin photo)

at big surf and reach an erroneous conclusion. They believe that fish have as much trouble in rough water as people do, but that just isn't accurate. Fish have evolved both the anatomy and physiology to handle big water almost effortlessly, while two-legged landlubbers are tossed, tumbled, and disoriented by even modest waves, sweeps, and surges.

Sheltered Venues:

Conditions are quite different in sheltered water spots, such as deep inside inlets, bays, harbors, and sounds where the water is usually calm. Still, larger sheltered waters such as big bays and sounds are also affected by storms and strong winds, and rough days pop up now and then.

Large or small, these sheltered locations are covered by one scientific descriptor: they are estuaries. There is a very important difference between big waves in the ocean and big waves in more confined bodies of water. The difference lies in the period of the waves, or the time interval between one wave and the next. The ocean is dominated by swells created by ocean storms with local winds overlaying a chop. Swells are longer period waves. Local wind driven waves dominate more confined waters such as sounds. These are short period waves. Why is this important to anglers? It is very difficult to make surface lure presentations in the short period wave mode. Short period waves are steep-sloped and narrow, and just as one crest passes another surges up behind it. On the other hand, longer period ocean waves have more gentle slopes and the wave itself is thicker from the trough to the crest, and on most occasions there is enough time between wave crests to get a surface lure to work properly. Frankly, I tend to fish sub-surface lures in rough surf whether the waves have a short or long period because gamefish prefer to hunt deep. They easily glide under the bottom or "foot" of the wave, out of the turbulence, and feed on baits that are tossed in the churning water. Therefore, I like to get down to the fish and make it easy for them to see and get to my lure. Therefore, bucktails and "tins" are my go-to lures in rough surf.

Staying In Touch:

One rule of thumb that can help an angler make good presentations in rough surf is to go bigger. That is, use bigger tackle, bigger sub-surface lures, and stay in touch with the lure. Staying in touch means the angler always "feels" the lure work. This is very important in wavy surf because the waves lift, push, and pull on the lure. Typically, a constant retrieve does not produce a consistent presentation. That's because the front of a wave pushes on the lure and creates slack in the line, while water on the back of the wave pulls on the lure and could cause the lure to spin or flop around. Savvy anglers "feel" the water tension on the lure and accelerate or decelerate the retrieve depending upon whether the "feel" goes slack or pulls tight.

Of course, it's a lot easier to stay in touch with a big swimmer because of the drag on the swimming lip. Bucktails and tins can be trickier, so when I fish with them I watch the line for fluctuations in line tension. In either case; the wobble of the lure, or the tension on the line, I stay in touch with the lure in an attempt to establish evenness in the retrieve. To recap: I sometimes must increase the speed of the retrieve and other times slow the retrieve or stop completely for a few seconds so that the lure's motion is consistent.

Lure presentation and release are easier in sheltered waters.

Productivity By Venue:

Okay, I've shown how calm and rough surf beaches have different personalities. You'd be correct if your next thought was that variations in conditions and beach structures causes productivity to vary too. The factors that control productivity are moon phases, winds and other weather, seasons, and beach structure. For example, spots that tend to be calmer tend to have more stable structure. Then too, the effects of the moon on tidal ranges can vary tremendously over a short distance depending upon whether we are considering the ocean or an estuary. The chart below summarizes the major factors that affect productivity in different venues.

Productivity Factors In Different Surf Venues

	Ocean	Estuaries (Special Estuaries)	Inlets	Jetties
Beach Structure:	unstable	stable	more or less stable	stable
Tide Effects:	minimal range	bigger ranges	tidal currents vital	eddies major
Moon Phases:	minimal impact	major impact	major impact	major impact
Seasons:	mostly autumn	mostly spring	spring/fall	all year

Applications:

Anglers, who understand and appreciate the differences in these factors and how they affect fishing from one venue type to another, are in a better position to make adjustments. For example, many excellent anglers concentrate their efforts in

Inlets typically have strong tidal currents that affect lure presentation and how we fight the fish. (Zeno Hromin photo)

bays, inlets, and larger estuaries in the spring, and then switch to the ocean beach in the fall. They know that the physical characteristics of these two types of fishing areas are different and they adjust by changing their tackle, lures, and presentations. Take another example: Tidal ranges in the more or less regular ocean basin vary much less than in some larger estuaries. That's because in the ocean, tide is the result of a periodic (rolling tide) wave that produces a minimal tidal range. However, over irregular basins with irregular shorelines a standing wave is established with greater tidal ranges. As a result, savvy anglers who fish in these spots wait for full and new moon phases when tidal ranges are large and extreme low tides concentrate bait schools and attract predators.

Typically, estuaries are calmer than oceans: but not always of course. An angler fishing in an estuary might forgo a foul weather top (although I recommend the use of a top for safety reasons) and a nine-foot stick because the water is calm, the fish closer, and lures smaller. That same angler working an ocean beach during the fall run, loads the bag with lures that are big, bigger, and biggest, and totes that eleven-foot stick wherever he goes. He or she tries to be prepared, both physically and mentally, for the forces generated by big waves along ocean beaches. In short, wave action rather than tides controls where bait goes and how fish feed.

Another example of applying knowledge to the unique aspects of a surf venue occurs in April in back waters. Many surf rats prefer the incoming tide on sunny days in April, even though it's the outgoing these anglers ply otherwise. That's because the sun warms the mud flats at low tide and in turn warms the water as it flows over the mud flats on the flood tide. Baitfish congregate over these flats in warmer water because the tiny food they eat also swims into the warm water. Of course, early spring stripers follow the same swim route onto the mud flats.

More:

In addition to variations in tidal range, shoreline topography, and depth, other differences contribute to how and when beaches produce. These are bottom structures, currents, and the speed at which water in these basins heats and cools.

Bottom Structures:

Rises and falls in the water basin not only affects tidal ranges it also affects how water flows within the basin. A sudden local rise in the bottom causes water to pile up on the up-tide side of the structure, water pressure increases, and ultimately the pressure is relieved when the water accelerates towards the surface creating a rip. Rips attract bait, creating condensed feeding opportunities that predators take advantage of.

Currents:

Obviously, currents, bottom structures, and irregular shorelines are all related. What might not be so obvious is that previously discussed factors such as moon phases will have an effect on the speed of the current and how turbulent it is. Some rips feature strong currents almost everyday, while others are strong around the moons and weak otherwise. Angler strategy includes fishing at rips when currents are strongest.

Temperature Changes:

Water heats and cools more slowly than air, and the larger the body of water the slower it heats and cools. That means shallow estuaries heat first in spring, plankton and bait spawn earlier, and the food chain gets a kick-start. As a result, fishing is better in the shallower water in spring. Conversely, fishing shuts down first in shallower bodies of water in autumn. Ocean blitzes often continue well into December in the ocean, while early November usually signals a shutdown in many shallow estuaries.

Chapter 5
CASTING AND RETRIEVING

In my view, too many newcomers to surf fishing as well as some experienced anglers, don't pay enough attention to the precision of their casting and retrieving. Yet, solid casting mechanics allow anglers to make accurate, longer casts that set up the lure for better presentations.

Believe it or not, good casting mechanics starts with the angler's stance and the equipment used. A baseball player in the batter's box may have a poor swing because he stands wrong, holds the bat wrong, and then twists his body awkwardly. So too will bad mechanics cause your casts to go all over the place. A bad start results in a bad cast, and poor casting reduces an angler's ability to catch fish. Just as a baseball player will not perform well using the branch of a tree for a bat, likewise an angler who uses equipment of poor quality or components that don't match will cast poorly. Even anglers with normally good casting mechanics will fall short with poor equipment. Worse perhaps is the tendency to overcompensate for poor tackle. That results in the development of bad habits that lead to bad casting mechanics.

At this point I'll refer you back to chapter two, *The Second Year*, for a discussion about the value of quality tools to use in the sport of surf fishing. If one compares rods and reels to automobiles, then a Mercedes is probably over-kill for many of us, a Mini Cooper a significant under-kill, while a Ford or Chevy SUV might be just right!

Hold The Rod Right: Please!

I have mentored new surf anglers for many years and take great pride in the fact that many have gone on to become top twenty finishers in the New York Surf Fishing Contest. From time to time a guy would ask me to be his mentor. Initially, I'd tell him that I'd watch him fish and think about it over the course of a few fishing trips. For several would-be students, I spotted something immediately that needed to be addressed: often it was how a guy held his surf rod. Some anglers are in the habit of holding the surf rod under their arm: in the armpit actually, and that, dear friends, is not how to hold a surf rod. I'll get around to the reasons for this in a minute. For now, what follows is a typical dialogue between my student and me.

"Put your rod between your legs where it belongs," I said.

"Okay," he said.

Two casts later, the angler had positioned the rod under the armpit again.

"I told you to put the rod between your legs." Pause. "Let me put this in another way. If you don't put that rod in your crotch and keep it there, I won't mentor you."

I relate this story to emphasize how important it is to use your tackle properly. That means the rod is in the crotch during the retrieve: no ands, ifs, or buts! That's where a good retrieve starts. Here are a few reasons why it's important.

1. When the rod butt is fixed in the crotch the butt can't swing up when a fish hits the lure or as you set the hook. When the rod-tip goes down and the butt up in the air, it's harder to sink a hook. The larger the fish, the harder it is to set a hook. When the butt is anchored, the tip goes down, the angler lifts up, and the hook is set. Simple!

2. When the rod is held under the armpit, the rod actually pivots on a fulcrum (balance point) directly under the hand that holds the rod. The rod acts like a seesaw. That's a vision I think we can all connect to unless there's somebody out there who never played on a seesaw. I find it hard to believe that there are guys out there that never played on a seesaw as a kid, so I'm comfortable making the reference. Pivoting across the handhold changes the action of the lure in the water and hence the presentation.

3. It is more difficult to stay in contact with a lure when the rod is held under the armpit because the "feel" of the tackle is distorted by the angle of the rod, the way the line enters the rod's tip-top, and because the pivoting action creates slack.

This angler demonstrates the proper way to hold a surf rod. (Zeno Hromin photo)

4. Holding a rod under your armpit is much more tiring on your wrist, fingers, shoulders, and your neck.
5. Fighting a fish with the rod under your arm is awkward. The angler has difficulty adjusting to the surges of a fighting fish, and loses much of the advantage of the length of the rod as a lever to control and land the fish.

Casting Mechanics:

Okay, let's assume at this point that the angler has quality tools, holds the rod properly with the rod butt in his crotch, and understands the basic physics of a rod and reel combination. With that assumption in place, we're ready to consider the cast. To explain casting mechanics, let's go back to the baseball player comparison. A batter needs balance, timing, and a swing rhythm. A caster needs the same things.

Balance:

Make sure that your body weight is evenly distributed over your legs. If there's a wobble or any sense of instability, reposition your feet. Stand so that you look down the beach: to the right if you're right handed, and to the left if you're left handed. Let's take the right-handed case. Your right foot should be slightly behind your body and the toes pointing towards the water at a 45-degree angle. Your left foot should be the same distance in front of your body so that the distance between your feet is about the width of your hips. Now, point the toes on your left foot in the direction you want your lure to go. Recheck your balance and make adjustments if needed. Now, lay the rod to your right and to the back. Your right arm will be extended back and your right elbow very slightly bent, while your left arm is bent significantly and the left elbow held close to your body. The rod should layout perpendicular to your body and parallel to the sand at the height of your waist. You are now positioned to begin the cast. However, before we cast, let's go back to our baseball batter.

Note the following features: The legs are bent and slightly apart, the right arm is extended, the left arm is bent at the elbow, and the angler rotates his upper body helping to propel the rod through an overhead arc.(Zeno Hromin photo)

When a batter swings he must stay back. That is, keep more weight on the rear leg. Then, when he begins the swing, his body moves forward first. He keeps his hands back. Shortly after the body shifts forward, he begins the process of clearing his hips (swiveling them towards the pitcher) and keeps his hands back. At the end of the hip clearing process the batter begins to rotate his shoulders towards the pitcher but continues to keep his hands back. Only when the body, hips, and shoulders are moving towards the pitcher (this develops the power of the swing), does the batter begin to swing with his arms by extending them and pulling the bat through the hitting zone with his hands. What many non-players don't realize about hitting is if you do all these things right you'll make contact with the ball slightly in front of the tip of home plate. If the batter pulls the ball through the zone well before the ball has arrived, the batter will miss the ball. On the other hand, if the bat is behind when the ball arrives, it's likely the batter will foul the pitch off. If the batter doesn't clear the hips and shoulders and only swings with the arms, the chances are the batter will not hit the ball hard or put it in play.

Similarly, a caster needs to begin the forward stride by lifting the left foot off the sand and gliding easily forward. The body moves in the same direction. Next, the caster must clear the hips, then the shoulders, and finally extend the arms and swing the rod. The rod should also point at the spot where the angler wants the lure to go as the left foot hits the sand and the line is released from the right index finger. Both batters and casters should follow through because it allows for maximum casting distance and accuracy. The difference between a batter and a caster is that a batter swings at waist level and the caster swings over his head and next to the right ear. At this point it's wise to remember that the follow through on a cast does not mean the angler should allow extra loops of line to come off the spool. These extra loops lead to "wind" knots and tangles and therefore one should never allow slack at the end of the cast. In fact, try to anticipate the lure hitting the water and stop the line from coming off the reel, either by placing a finger against the spool, picking up the line with the index finger, or by closing the bail.

Most experienced surf anglers prefer manual rollers over reel bails. (Zeno Hromin photo)

Bails or Manual Rollers:

That reminds me to discuss the choice between using a reel with only a roller or one with a bail. Let me begin by pointing out that with only a little practice anyone can become comfortable with a manual system and within ten or twenty minutes. However, to get to a comfort level, an angler needs to avoid a few pitfalls that can lead to bad habits. It's much easier to start right than to change bad habits. The pitfalls are first, looking at your fingers and at the reel. Properly done, this is a process done by feel and not by eye. Looking at the reel and your fingers to pick up line and put it on the roller takes too much time and leads to wind knots and other difficulties. Second, don't switch hands. That is, don't manipulate the line with one hand and hold the rod with the other, or switch the hand that holds the rod. Third, make sure your reel hand is in the correct position. Here's how I handle it.

I put the stem of the reel between my fourth finger and my pinky (9-11 foot outfits). I move the line roller to a position closest to the rod. I extend my index finger and using a snatching motion, I grab the line and move it off the roller and towards the rod. Now I make the cast. I allow the line to slip off my finger when the rod tip points at the eleventh hour on an imaginary clock dial. Another way to say this is to see the rod tip pointing into the air in front of you and slightly forward of center, or forward of a point directly above your head. Just before the lure hits the water, I extend my index finger and the line becomes caught on the tip of the finger, and this stops loops of line from coming off the spool. Now, I pull the line toward the rod blank with my index finger and begin reeling. As the roller makes a pass close to the rod, it picks up the line because you have put the line in the path of the roller. Straighten your finger as you feel a pull as the line moves onto the roller. Now, quickly release the hand holding the rod at the reel stem and slide it up onto the rod's fore grip. Finally, slide the rod between your legs. All done, just retrieve.

I don't like bails because the spring that pulls the bail arm over the top of the spool has a limited life expectancy. Springs have only so many stretches before they are weakened and snap. Even if you close the bail with your hand, the spring uncoils and coils. Typically, they snap at the worst time. I also don't like the bail because it's in the way and I sometimes get my knuckles banged as the bail arm passes around the spool. The rollers on bail arms are also too small for my liking. Manual systems have fewer moving parts, there are no springs to snap, the roller is bigger and stronger, and it is really easy to learn to use a bail-less system, in spite of what you might think. But, if you must use a bail, the same casting principles apply, and it is important to avoid extra line loops coming off the spool after the lure has hit the water.

Once again, whether we talk about break-offs, bird nests, loops, tangles, faulty casts, or tackle problems, the truth remains that we cause these issues. There is no point in cursing at the reel, the line, the rod, the lure, or the wind because the cause can almost always be found by looking in the mirror.

Summary Points:

1. Place the rod between your legs where it belongs for best results.
2. Pay attention to your casting mechanics.
3. Manual rollers are superior to bails and very easy to get accustomed to.
4. Anglers cause most tackle problems, or at least we contribute significantly to the result.
5. A smooth easy motion usually results in longer casts than an extra forceful jerky thrusting motion.

Chapter 6
LINE STUFF: KNOTS, LEADERS, & TEASERS

I follow the K.I.S.S. principle when it comes to equipment and fishing. By the way, K.I.S.S. stands for *keep it simple stupid*. Because I follow this principle, my knots are simple, my leaders simple, my terminal hardware readily available, and my teasers cost pennies, not dollars. Yes, I believe in being fastidious about my tackle, but exotic knots, and five-dollar teasers don't fall into my definition of fastidious. Too many anglers, in my opinion, get too wrapped up in the misinformation that insists anglers use one specific knot, one style of leader, and one type of fancy teaser. Let's keep it simple and have more fun.

Knots:

Let's go over the knot issue again because it is such an important one. I use only one knot to tie my braided line to the swivel on my leader. It is the improved clinch knot. It is simple, easy to tie, can be tied in the dark, and if tied correctly is a knot of 95% of the line's rated strength. I've heard so-called experts, even on television shows, rattle on about how anglers can't use an improved clinch knot with braid. Well, I must be a very lucky guy because it's the only knot I tie and I have no problems with it.

I even saw a test of knots on a popular television show and the improved clinch knot failed against other knots that the narrator openly proclaimed to be rather difficult to tie. The truth is the knot didn't fail, the show's host failed. He failed to account for the slippery nature of braided line compared to monofilament or fluorocarbon lines. Whereas, one makes five or six turns when tying a knot with monofilament line, one must make nine or ten turns with braid. Also, make sure to pull against the tag end of the line as well as the running line when cinching up the knot. If the knot is properly tied there are no loops, no overlays of turns and no bulges. Discard and retie if any of these things happen. By the way, most exotic knots have a rated knot strength of between 80 and 90% of the line's strength, and are much more cumbersome to tie.

I also use a Uni-knot to connect my monofilament backing on the reel to the braided front line. I use it because it is a reliable knot for tying two different materials together. It is not as easy to tie as the improved clinch knot, but neither a blood knot (traditionally used to connect mono to mono) or an improved clinch knot is appropriate to connect different kinds of lines or lines of different thickness. Since I don't need to tie the Uni-knot very often, I don't feel oppressed by the increased difficulty of tying a proper one.

Leaders provide a measure of safety and convenience when landing and unhooking the fish.

Leader Vs. Shock Leader:

Many anglers, mostly old timers, still use a shock leader. A shock leader was developed a long time ago to give surf anglers a casting edge because distance is often so important. Typically, the angler would spool up using fifteen-pound test monofilament line and attach fifteen feet or so of thirty or forty-pound test monofilament line to the main line. The length of the shock leader depended on the length of the rod, but when ready to cast, anglers liked to have at least three or four turns of shock leader on the spool.

The heavy shock leader took the brunt of the forceful cast while the thinner main line allowed for longer casts. Some anglers prefer the shock leader at night, pointing out that the knot comes through the guides easily whereas barrel swivels clunk through the tip-top and have a propensity of cracking the tip-top. I've found that if the length of a snap and swivel leader is appropriate to the length of the rod, I don't reel the swivel through the tip-top. So, I don't use a shock leader. Also, anglers should be paying attention to their tackle and not daydreaming.

Braided lines and better reels and rods have made the shock leader superfluous in my opinion. I use a length of Perlon leader material. This is a stiff nylon material that's tough as nails. It can even stand up to bluefish teeth for a while and it's sold in forty-inch lengths. I tie these leaders with a 75-pound Tactical Anglers paperclip style snap on the lure end and a number five or seven barrel swivel on the main line end of the leader. The length will vary depending on the size of the rod. I like eighteen to twenty-two inches for my nine-foot outfit and thirty inches for my eleven-foot outfit. Don't buy into the following myth: Fish shy away from Perlon and heavy monofilament leaders. Actually, in our turbid and plankton rich waters, the fish simply don't notice and don't care. Now, should I make a trip to the gin-clear waters of the Bahamas, I'll be sure to take along a spool of fluorocarbon to use as leaders. I've been using a snap with a swivel and short leaders for decades with success. You might want to consider that if there were any advantage to using mono or fluorocarbon line, I would use it because I can't abide poor angling results. I've competed for many years and therefore I'd never surrender any advantage that was available. Modern materials and equipment actually relegates the leader to a role of safety and convenience. Keep it simple!

Swivels and Snaps:

I have already indicated my preference for Tactical Angler paperclip snaps and barrel swivels. At one time I used Duo-Lock snaps (# 54 & 55), but the paperclip styles have won me over in recent years. Also don't be put off by the size of a number seven-barrel swivel. It may look small and breakable,

The new paperclip style snaps are strong and provide the most secure terminal connection. (Alberto Knie photo)

but the good brands have a breaking strength of 75 pounds. Unless you're planning to catch a blue marlin, seventy-five pounds of strength is more than enough for the tackle we use and the fish we catch.

Again, I use an improved clinch knot to tie both the snap and swivel to the leader material. Keep it simple!

Strength Of Leader:

I use thirty-pound test Perlon most of the time. Occasionally, if I'm fishing in rocky areas or in very rough surf that's loaded with suspended sand, I'll switch to forty-pound test Perlon. This is very tough material and can take lots of abuse from abrasion, gill covers, and even teeth.

Wire Leaders:

I learned my lesson four decades ago while fishing with my friend Bob Krauss. He never used a wire leader even when fishing for blues. He was rarely bit off, rarely lost either fish or lures because of the heavy-duty nylon leader and he out-fished me regularly. One day we had a chat about it, his arguments were powerful, and he convinced me to not use wire leaders when fishing with lures, and I never did again. He argued that the wire was more visible, made more bubbles along with the swivel, and was too easily kinked. Kinking reduces the strength of the wire significantly.

Teasers:

I'm selective about my use of teasers. I don't use them extensively day and night the way many anglers do, and for good reasons. First, there's the issue of bluefish. Decades ago I lost some nice plugs and big fish because a large blue spotted my teaser and plug and hit the teaser from the side. That's right, you figured it out. I lost the entire kit and caboodle. Second, I've had bad experiences when two nice fish were on at once: one on the teaser and one on the lure. Inevitably, they swim in opposite directions, shake their heads in synchrony, and snap the leader. The third reason involves the weakness of the teaser connection to the main leader. A dropper loop is a 50% knot: and that's not enough strength for me. I've tried attaching the teaser to the barrel swivel of the leader, but that didn't work well either because of a strong tendency for the teaser's short leader to wrap around the main leader, again and again. When the teaser wraps around the leader a proper presentation is impossible. At one point, I developed a teaser leader approach with a very strong one-piece leader using a knot taught to me by a friend. I tied it so that the teaser loop and the main leader were one continuous piece of leader material. That solved the tangling problem and the knot strength issue, but did not address the bluefish issue or the double fish snap problem. That's when I decided that catching one fish at a time was enough.

That said, I do use teasers selectively. For example, I use them at night, in the spring, when gamefish feed on small sand eels. I also tie on a teaser in late fall, after the bluefish are gone, if there's a late ocean run of schoolies. Except for those two limited uses, I avoid them because they are usually more trouble than they're worth. That's just one man's opinion because many experienced anglers use teasers on a regular basis with great success. As I've previously explained, there are several ways to attach the teaser to the main leader. If the ones I've mentioned don't strike your fancy, consult anyone of a number of sources from the Internet to books, for other choices, and then pick your poison. Let's move on to a discussion about teasers.

Red Gill:

Red Gill teasers have been a favorite among surf anglers for decades. A one point, they were sold just about everywhere, but changing marketing terms and conditions have made it difficult for some smaller outlets to carry them. However, I'm told they can be purchased online, but it may be more convenient to purchase them from The Surfcaster in Darien Connecticut. Their latest catalogue has a variety of sizes and colors for sale.

Generally, we use the smaller ones in spring and the larger ones in the fall. They are remarkably durable and have a paddle tail that makes the skinny plastic body wiggle. They are most effective at night in quiet water, when stripers hunt small sand eels or spearing in shallow water.

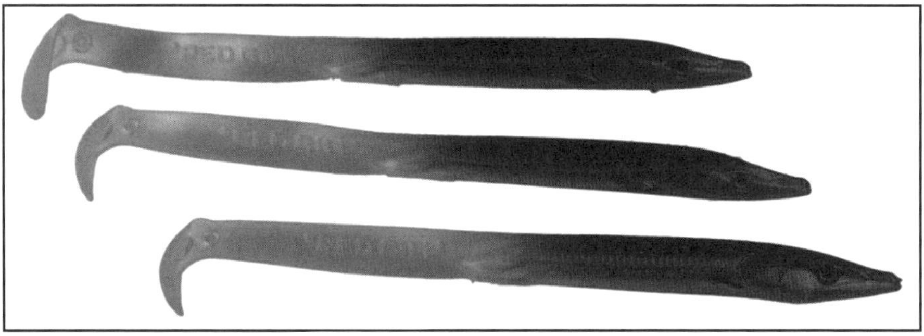

Red Gill plastics are among the most popular and effective teasers.

Feather Teasers:

Perhaps the most popular teasers are the feather models because they are readily available, inexpensive, effective, and durable. Most anglers tend to use three and four-inch feather teasers in spring, and six and seven-inch teasers in the fall. Feather teasers, and bucktail teasers too, can also imitate stocky bodied baits such as peanut bunker, small butterfish, herring, and sardines, young of the year shapes such as snappers and weakfish, as well as sand eels. The imitation of larger baits is made possible by the characteristics of feathers and bucktail hair. Bucktail hair is hollow and allows the teaser to "breathe." That is, the hairs puff out and collapse as the teaser move through the water. The profile of the teaser is large when puffed up. Hackle feathers can be tied in a variety of ways: lean and full. For instance, when cinder worms hatch and fish get fussy, I tie two three-inch lengths of hot pink hackle feathers on a 3/0 stainless steel hook and use this as the teaser. The small thin profile and pink color (copying one of the colors of cinder worms) make it possible for me to at least pick a few nice stripers. On the other side of the coin, I tie on ten or twelve six-inch long white feathers on a 3/0 stainless steel hook for the fall run in an effort to create the illusion of short, deep-bodied baits. That is, if I choose to use a teaser at all.

Summary:

1. Apply the K.I.S.S. principle. Keep it simple, decrease the chances of problems, and increase your success.
2. Knots: The improved clinch knot is easy to tie and the knot boasts 95% of the line's pound-test rating when tied correctly. Use a Uni-Knot for connecting the monofilament backing on your reel to the main braided line.
3. I use a 20-30-inch leader. It provides anglers with a measure of safety, convenience when unhooking fish, and an easy way to change a lure. For most situations I use 30-40 pound test leader material.
4. Leaders are constructed with at least a 75-pound test paperclip style snap on the lure end and either a number 5 or 7-barrel swivel on the running line end of the leader.
5. No wire leaders, please!
6. Teasers can be effective when attached to the leaders and used with the main lure, but I'm very choosy about when I use them. Some choices include small plastic styles, feathers, and bucktail teasers.

Chapter 7
LURES THAT CATCH FISH: BUCKTAILS

The Best All-Around:

It's my opinion of course, and some might differ with my thesis, but since I'm writing this book I get to offer my opinion. I won't go into bucktailing in great detail in this chapter because I recently wrote a book, *Fishing With Bucktails*, devoted exclusively to the topic. The book is available in many stores, catalogues, and online too. Therefore, I believe it is a better use of this space if I review my reasons for using bucktails and why I believe these hairy jigs are the best all-around lures.

Bucktails are effective on larger bass because the angler can work them deep where the big ones lurk.(Drew Muller photo)

My History:

There was a time, decades ago, when I didn't fish with bucktails at all. Like many of you I didn't trust the lures so I didn't fish with them. Sure, I'd read about them and heard other anglers speak about how many fish they caught with bucktails, but when I looked at the lures I didn't see much to get excited about. Unlike beautifully painted life-like plugs that wiggled, rolled, and popped, bucktails didn't look like any baitfish

I'd ever seen. When I pulled them through the water they didn't seem to do much, either. My bucktails remained in my bag and gradually rusted to the point where they were useless. That is until that fateful day when I first met my now good friend John Skinner and he put on a fish-catching show with bucktails the likes of which I had never seen. From that day on, I became a bucktail angler.

Got Over My Fear:

I realized that I was prejudiced against bucktails. I realized I was afraid to use them. I realized I didn't know how to use them. I realized I had no confidence in the lure. Last but not least, I realized that I had a lot of work to do and a choice to make. The choice was between learning to use the lure or not. The work was to practice, think, read, observe, and try until I overcame my fears.

I won't lie, my journey to success took a while. But then again, it took a while to learn how to fish with poppers too, and shiny metal lures, plastic swimmers, metal-lipped swimmers, and every other lure that I ultimately mastered. But it was abundantly clear to me at the time that the bucktail held the potential to add significantly to my success. So, I got on the horse and never looked back. Sure, at first I lost plenty of bucktails to rocks and bottom debris. I struggled to find a rhythm, experimented with retrieve speeds and hook embellishments, and worked hard to figure out the relationship between water depth, waves, and currents, and the size and style of the bucktail. I learned the hard way that if I didn't fish the lures properly, I didn't catch much. Over time, I learned to select the right size, and use the proper embellishment. At the time, there was very little available to help me in my progress. You're luckier than I was, because If you want to learn how to fish with bucktails, you have at your disposal a vast array of information on the subject from many sources.

Basics:
Who's Bucktail Should I Use:

I have nothing against the Spro bucktail, and it is very popular. Hell, I use them almost exclusively for fluke fishing. However, I offer this discussion because so many new beach rats are drawn to use them for gamefish. In my view, there are better bucktail choices for stripers, blues, and weakfish. Why? The hook on the Spro bucktail isn't forged steel, and more than one big bass or blue has straightened these hooks during the fight. Second, the Spro bucktail has a tendency to flop around in rough and turbulent water. Third, the ties around the hair aren't as durable as those from other manufacturers.

For example, I use Uncle Josh bucktails because they boast a pot belly design, a strong tie on the hair that's secured with epoxy glue, have thick stainless steel hangers that don't rust, bend or wear through. The bucktails come with a 3X strong

I prefer swing hook bucktails such as those made by Uncle Josh and I always add a strip of pork rind.

forged hooks and the Uncle Josh bucktail is a swing hook design. The swing hook has advantages. One, I can easily change the hook when it starts to rust. I use Mustad 34091 D or ED trailer hooks as replacements. These are open-eye hooks that can be closed quickly and easily on the hanger, they are relatively inexpensive, and they are strong and durable.

Size:

Let me get you started with a few simple basic elements and ideas. Initially buy a few bucktails in the three-quarter to one and a half-ounce size range. These are the basic sizes that will cover your needs in ninety percent of fishing situations. Don't even try to use very small or very heavy bucktails until you have had considerable success with the basic sizes.

Color:

I recommend white bucktails and only white, while anglers are learning to use the lures. It's simpler that way and, since all fish have white bellies and/or sides, you will not be at a significant disadvantage. Using other colors can wait until you are comfortable and successful using basic bucktails, and proficient in using them.

Style:

There are many styles of bucktails from flat-bottom styles, to flat-sided ones, to round head types, to pot belly styles, and they all have their day, but for my money the pot belly style is the best all-around shape because it runs true, holds position in wavy water, and never spins.

Porkrind:

I use Uncle Josh red and white model 240-S porkrind as hook embellishments. Although anglers will catch fish on bucktails without any embellishment (naked), you'll generally catch more fish by adding something to the bucktail hook. Many anglers like to use plastic curly tail embellishments, but they are easily ripped by stripers and chopped by blues. They add action, but

I don't think it's always the right "look," and replacing torn ones takes too much time away from catching fish. I settled on pork rind a long time ago. I guess my view is validated by the legions of experienced and successful anglers who opt for porkrind over other embellishments for bucktails, just as I do.

Retrieves:

Keep the retrieves basic until you start to catch fish regularly with bucktails. First, don't drag or bounce bucktails on the bottom. That's a terrific approach for fluke, but for stripers, blues, and weakfish, not so much. For most applications, try to keep the bucktail within one or two feet of the bottom because that's where gamefish spend most of their time as they move and feed. Surface feeding accounts for only a small percentage of feeding behavior. Most of the time fish feed unseen below the surface. Don't jig the bucktail wildly. The best bucktail anglers I know generally retrieve slow and steady within one to two feet of the bottom. They do use other approaches from time to time, but that's not the way to begin your journey. Remember that a good bucktail angler has put many miles on his or her feet, and many tides under his or her belt. Keep it simple until you are comfortable with your success, and then begin to think about advanced retrieves. It is important to remain patient while you learn. You can read this, you can read my bucktail book, and although you'll gain a big edge, there are things about "feel" I can't describe. I'd love to be able to teach you about "feel," but in reality it's the part of the technique that becomes focused only with practice. Be patient and stick with your bucktail learning curve. Enjoy the learning curve. Once mastered, the curve can never be enjoyed again.

The Significance:

I guess I sound like a former smoker who, after quitting the habit, goes around enthusiastically preaching that others should stop smoking too, but that isn't the case. My enthusiasm comes from the knowledge that bucktails match all kinds of baitfish, catch virtually every gamefish that swims, and can be fished in all levels of the water column. The value of bucktails as fish-catchers is reflected in my angling life. I use bucktails 80-90% of the time. I'm not trying to prove a point. Rather I'm interested in catching fish. Typically, a bucktail is the first lure I put on my snap, and it's still there when I go home: that's how powerful the lure is. Sure, I use other lures: swimmers, poppers, pencil poppers, tins, and swim baits. I use them all, but I only do so when conditions or the fish tell me there's a better choice than a bucktail. Bucktails are also lures that I can use anywhere: in the ocean, the bays, inlets, over sand, around rocks, off jetties, and on mud flats too. I regret all the years before I met John Skinner, when I didn't fish with bucktails and he wasn't yet my friend.

Although I generally use white bucktails, green is an excellent choice under certain conditions. (Zeno Hromin photo)

Summary:

1. Employ the K.I.S.S. principle. That is, *keep it simple stupid*.
2. Get over your fear of bucktails, because it's worth the effort.
3. Style: Uncle Josh potbelly, swing hook models are the ones I use.

4. Size: ¾ to 1 and ½-ounce bucktails cover 90% of situations.
5. Color: Use only white during the early stages of your learning curve.
6. Embellishment: I use porkrind (red and white, model 240-S) on my bucktails.
7. Retrieves: Low and slow, no violent jigging.
8. Significance: Bucktails catch all species under almost all conditions.
9. For more information on the subject read, *Fishing With Bucktails.*

Chapter 8 LURES THAT CATCH FISH: PENCIL POPPERS

Why They Work So Well:

Pencil poppers are basically daytime surface lures that are retrieved with what's called a "walk the dog" action. Walking the dog is an erratic side-to-side retrieve, first introduced with the freshwater Zara Spook lure. In the 21st Century there are a variety of surface stick bait lures on the market for freshwater use, and they all boast the "walk the dog" surface motion. These freshwater models catch fish too, but aren't durable enough for saltwater monsters.

The idea of a floating teardrop shaped lure, designed to be retrieved with a "walk the dog" action, was applied to saltwater gamefish in the 20th Century. These new style poppers became known as pencil poppers and soon were very popular among the new breed of surf fishermen that emerged after World War II.

Companies like **Gibbs** began producing a variety of wood lures because of a growing interest in coastal states such as Massachusetts, Rhode Island, and New York. Among the lures were two types of poppers: the conventional style **Polaris** popper and the **Pencil Popper**. Gibbs pencil poppers remain very popular and come in the standard series and the Pro Series. **Atom** also makes several sizes of pencil poppers, and these lures are made from compressed plastic. Cotton Cordell makes plastic extruded pencil poppers in one and two-ounce sizes. The Cordell pencils have rattles: a big plus, in my opinion, but they do not cast as well as the other models and, because they don't "sit" well in rough water, are better suited to calm backwater locations.

There are also pencil poppers that were developed for saltwater by "cottage industry" style companies. These handcrafted pencils were much stronger than freshwater 3/8th-ounce stick baits. Whether produced by Gibbs or a local artisan, they

Pencil poppers such as this Yo-Zuri Surface Cruiser are effective because they mimic wounded baitfish struggling on the surface. (Zeno Hromin photo)

generally weigh between two and four ounces for long casts, boast large profiles for large gamefish, and are through-wired for strength.

In the mid Twentieth Century, surf rats soon discovered that pencil poppers imitated a variety of wounded saltwater baitfish, including bunker, herring, mackerel, butterfish, and a variety of young of the year fish too. Wood pencil poppers became wildly popular in the latter years of the 20th century, and remain very popular today. There are still many pencils available in wood, because many anglers prefer some of the unique qualities of wood that plastic cannot copy. However, there is no denying that plastic offers the opportunity for a more consistent product, as well as the opportunity to add rattles. Beach anglers also discovered that the slow side-to-side motion of pencil poppers triggered strikes in calm waters when fish were not feeding intensely and often snubbed their noses at standard poppers.

To Be Fast, Or Not To Be Fast:

As Hamlet might say, yes, that is the question. Many anglers automatically retrieve pencil poppers rapidly, assuming that is "the" retrieve. However, pencil poppers may be retrieved in a variety of ways. Experienced seasoned anglers understand this and have studied the art of pencil popping carefully in order to get the most out of the lures.

In general, fast intense retrieves are best for bluefish: a fish that often, but not always, exhibits predator-prey responses more like those of a lion than a fish. That is, blues can often be triggered to attack something that moves fast. It's an instinctive response to motion, is coded in their DNA, and reflects their open-ocean life style. For example, a well-fed big cat might attack a fleeing small animal that it would otherwise ignore if the prey remained still. In another example, park rangers tell visitors not to run from a bear should they suddenly stumble upon one, because running triggers an attack even when the bear has just eaten.

Modern poppers are more easily presented with today's graphite rods. (Zeno Hromin photo)

Striped Bass and the Deliberate Mode:

Although there are days when stripers will chase pencil poppers retrieved at warp speed, that's the exception and not the rule. Stripers are usually opportunity feeders and, like it or not, the bigger bass get, the lazier they get. A big striper would much prefer a wounded slow moving food item to a healthy speedy one. Why? A large striper can eat almost anything it wants, almost anytime it wants. Therefore, why should the fish waste energy chasing something that's moving away quickly? I attempt to take advantage of this casual and lazy feeding style by retrieving pencils slowly and deliberately. I do not frantically whip the tip-top either; rather I induce a sluggish "walk the dog," side-to-side motion.

Old Days:

In the "old" days when all we had were fiberglass rods, we had to use a lot of effort with our arms and shoulders to entice a pencil into a rhythmic action. Boy, we tired so fast that in the absence of a strike or two most anglers switched to other lures in order to "take a break." I often secretly wished that the fish wouldn't be interested in pencil poppers on a given day, because I so dreaded the resulting pain. However, today's graphite rods are much better suited to pencil popping. A medium power, medium action surf rod allows an angler to work a pencil for long periods with very little effort. Most of the time, I use only my wrist in a gentle motion to get the pencil revved into action. I love modern fishing materials. Add non-stretching braided line and the process is as close to effortless as one can get.

Irregularity:

Although I begin with a steady easy retrieve, I move on to other motions if the fish don't respond. Of course, this assumes I have reasons to believe that stripers are present, and willing to feed at the surface. I think you already know my lure of choice when fish run deep. Enough said! Okay, this is the place where I will discuss an irregular retrieve. Begin with a standard slow and steady retrieve, and then stop once in a while. Or, begin

Stripers often hit a pencil popper after a miss if the angler pauses the retrieve for a second or two before resuming. (Zeno Hromin photo)

with a slow retrieve and introduce brief periods of frantic surface action before returning to a deliberate retrieve. Repeat the process of changing the action during the retrieve. If neither of these presentations induces strikes, I begin to assume that the fish either aren't around or are not feeding.

Or, if you continue to believe that stripers or blues are around, try changing the size of the pencil. I usually begin with a medium size pencil (approximately 2 ounces), and change to a smaller lure if the medium plug is ignored. However, moving up the weight ladder sometimes works too, especially during the fall run. It is true in freshwater and also in saltwater, that one of the ways to induce strikes from reluctant fish is to "down-size" your lure.

One piece of advice here is that color rarely makes a difference. Yes, it can during mullet runs, but most of the time color is not very important. Therefore, alter the retrieve and change size, but forget about a color change, because it's a last resort. Bouncing from one color to another distracts the angler from focusing on presentations.

The Pause That Refreshes:

Stripers have an annoying habit of toying with surface lures when they aren't in a positive feeding mode. They may swirl close to a surface lure, roll over it, make a mock splash behind it, or they may just follow it and push a wake of water. If these things happen, you'll be better off if you switch to a bucktail or tin.

However, if the bass actually hit the lure but miss, try this tip that might allow you to catch more fish, more often than not. It takes a bit of discipline to pull it off, but it's worth practicing and being prepared for. The instant you know the fish has missed the hook, pause and count off two seconds before restarting the retrieve. Typically, as soon as the pencil begins to move again, the striper will slam it and this time they rarely miss. The reason the pause works so well is because it's a match to how stripers feed on surface baits.

Cotton Cordell one ounce pencil poppers are among my favorites for quiet waters.

How They Feed:

Let's compare how a blue usually hits a surface lure and how a striper does it. Blues usually move fast towards a lure, slam it, and if they miss they either immediately slash at it again and again, or move away. Stripers typically approach surface baits slowly from below, and size them up. They rarely run a lure down from behind, preferring to come up from below. Once they decide to hit the lure, they will move to the surface and turn in a curved path as they approach the lure. As they pass the lure they suck it in, clamp down, and continue to turn towards the bottom. However, if they miss the hook, they will continue to move in a curve until they come full-circle and are looking up at the surface again. This takes about two seconds. At this point they reacquire the lure, and if it moves, their instinctive understanding is that they hit and wounded the bait, and it is now vulnerable. When the lure begins to move again it triggers an intense predator-prey response, and they hit the lure hard.

When To Use:

I prefer smaller plastic pencils such as the ⅞ ounce Atom pencil, the Cotton Cordell 1-ounce pencil, Tsunami's ⅞ ounce TS Talkin' Popper, Yo-Zuri's 1 ⅜ ounce Surface Cruiser, and Tactical Angler's SeaPencil in the spring and in quieter waters such as the backs of estuaries or along the shorelines of sounds and harbors. Plastic pencils with rattles are incredibly effective in calm water and I never leave home without a few in my bag. In the fall and in the ocean, I switch to heavier styles like the Gibbs 2 ⅜ ounce and 3 ½ ounce models, the Atom 2-ounce pencil, Tactical Angler's 2 ounce SeaPencil, and Tsunami's 2 ¼ ounce Talkin' Popper, and the Yo-Zuri 2 ⅛ ouncc and 3 ½ ounce Surface Cruiser. I generally carry mostly white ones, blue and white, or yellow and white versions. I really don't fuss over color. Long casts are needed in the ocean surf and lighter pencils such as the Cordell models don't cast nearly as far as the bigger models and they don't "sit" in the waves well either. In short, lighter plastic pencils are more difficult to cast and it is also harder to present them properly in rough water.

Summary:

1. Use smaller plastic pencil poppers in quiet water and bigger wood ones along ocean beaches.
2. Graphite rods and braided lines make what was formally the backbreaking chore of pencil popping easy.
3. Alter retrieve patterns when fish are reluctant feeders.
4. Downsize the pencil popper when fish are reluctant feeders.
5. When a fish hits the lure but misses, employ the "pause that refreshes" for an extra chance to catch the fish.
6. Don't fuss over color. It's the last thing I worry about.

Chapter 9
LURES THAT CATCH FISH: STANDARD POPPERS

Ancient, But Still Deadly:

Standard or conventional style poppers have been around a long time. They are basically daytime lures that mimic prey that swims at the surface. Saltwater forms evolved from freshwater models, but beefed up of course. Poppers are long cigar-shaped surface lures with a thin neck and a fat head with a scoped out face. The lure is designed to push and splash water. In the process, the lure makes a sound. Some actually make a popping sound and that's how the name, "popping" plug, originated. Other styles make a swooshing sound. Popping plugs imitate almost any kind of wounded bait struggling at the surface, and this is an important point for anglers to remember when they retrieve these poppers. Although speedy retrieves work well on occasion, wounded fish aren't speedy, and so a presentation that mimics the slow struggles of a vulnerable bait is usually much more effective than a loud, speedy, hectic retrieve. Although I will pop them strongly in rough water and when fish are feeding actively at the surface in order to attract attention, my everyday retrieve is a kind of a slosh as I try to create the illusion of an easy meal.

Size and Design Features:

Poppers come in many sizes from a fraction of an ounce to over four ounces. Obviously the heavier the popper the more effort is needed to make them pop. Many anglers believe that the bigger the popper the farther they will cast, but that's not always true. Casting distance is about the weight of the lure, how the weight is distributed, and the lure's aerodynamic qualities. Weight is the everyday on-earth word for mass, and bigger mass has more momentum than lesser mass, but if the weight isn't distributed in a specific way, the lure will tend to wiggle from side to side in the air instead of flying out tail first in a straight line. Weight distribution combined with the design of the lure's shape creates an aerodynamic lure. Lures designed without consideration of aerodynamic qualities tend to thrust out quickly, but then wobble, and as they wiggle in mid air, they experience air resistance. At this point, the lure loses momentum quickly to the friction generated by the board-side surface area contact with air. Models designed to be aerodynamic are weight-balanced so that the rear end of the plug forces its way through the air and does not wobble. The surface area of the end of the plug is much smaller than the sides and the lure can cut through the air when cast correctly. Strategically, designers place small weights in poppers in order to balance the lure both aerodynamically and hydro-dynamically. That is, create a lure that casts well and also moves properly in the water. Designing a "great" popper is as much an art as it is a science. Only the best lure designers get it right consistently.

Low light conditions at dawn and dusk enhance the effectiveness of large poppers. (Ross Squire photo)

Design can also be used to make a popper swim between pops thus generating splash, noise, and a swimming motion. Each time a lure adds an additional triggering or alluring dimension, it increases the likelihood of a strike. Poppers that swim are being increasing used during night tides, when long casts are imperative. Night use has therefore generated a surge of interest in night colors such as black, purple, purple and black, brown, and dark green or blue. These very dark hues were rarely seen prior to the adaptation of popping plugs to night feeding fish.

Head Styles:

At one time the heads of all poppers had more or less the same shape. Sure, there were minor differences, but the size of the scoped head could best be described as "medium" in size and did not seem out of ratio to the body of the plug. In other words, the size of the head and the body of the plug seemed to match well.

Then there was a major innovation: the bull-nose popper. This is a popping plug with an exaggerated wide head and a deep scope. Bull-nose plugs push more water and make more noise. More noise and splash can be effective when background noise and commotion tend to overwhelm the noise and commotion of the regular shaped head popper.

Plastic or Wood:

The controversy over which material makes the best lure has been active for many decades. Each material has its devotees, and the anglers in each camp are enthusiastic in their opinions and their choices.

Wood is a living material, it has pores, it has variations in density, and it floats. I admit this about wood, when I've gotten my hands on a special swimmer or popper made of wood, the productivity level of that particular lure was incredible. Some were so productive I retired them to a place of honor on my wall, rather than continue to use them because I was afraid of losing the plug. Yes, wood lures are like the little girl with the curl. That is, when they are good, they are very, very good, but when they are bad they are very, very bad. There are definitely clunkers among wood plugs. Years ago, some of the best anglers could detect the good ones from the bad just by eye and feel. Others would swim them in a pool, pond, or along the beach spotting those lures with just the right action, and the clunkers that didn't have a chance.

Most anglers find that plastic poppers offer consistent effectiveness, yet wooden poppers still have loyal fans. (Zeno Hromin photo)

One thing about lures made of plastic; they are of consistent quality. Some anglers argue that plastic limits the chance for that "home run" great plug, but on the other hand there aren't many clunkers either. There's no doubt about the high level of quality control in a production run of plastic plugs.

Cost has also driven plug manufacturers to use plastic. Making lures from wood that can sell at reasonable prices has become a challenge but, although plug making is an expensive process regardless of the materials used, plastic provides manufacturers with a little wiggle room when it comes to price.

New Cottage Industry - Plug Makers:

There's a philosophy out there that says everything comes around full circle. In the early decades after WW II most great plug designers worked independently. They turned the wood, weighted the plug, added the hardware, and sold the product of their efforts locally. As with all things, big business and rising costs forced many of these designers either out of business, or to expand their operation. The switch to plastic, several decades ago, added the last nail in the coffin for many of these local entrepreneurs. However, as stated previously, there are anglers devoted to wood plugs, and so, as the prices of plastic models increased, cottage-style plug making has had a renaissance along the striper coast. There are so many local plug brands now that I must admit I'm only familiar with a few. That said, friends who favor one of these models or the other tell me that the quality is good, action is consistent, and the poppers are productive.

Brands and Models:

Without question, Super Strike Little Neck Poppers are my favorite standard poppers. Don Musso is the founder of this company and a master lure designer. He's been designing plugs for a number of decades and he's one of the few local artisans to make the transition from wood to plastic without missing a beat. I use the 2 ⅜ ounce model most often because it casts so well, swims between pops, and can be comfortably worked under a variety of sea conditions. I suspect I use the 1 ½ ounce model almost as often as the medium size, but I only use the 3-ounce model in the fall when a large profile popper with a big splash is required. Again I affirm that I'm not big on color. I use white poppers most often, but will frequently go to Super Strike's blue and white poppers during a mullet run. Other colors are popular among surf anglers, including yellow and white, green and white, and chartreuse.

Super Strike Little Neck Poppers are among my favorites because they are tough, reliable and will swim when retrieved slowly. (Zeno Hromin photo)

Other popular models includes the Atom Striper Swiper, the Gibbs Polaris, the Yo-Zuri 3½-ounce Surface Bull and Sashimi Bull 150 popper, Tsunami's TS Talkin' popper, and the Tactical Angler 4 ounce BombPopper. There are a number of less expensive commercially produced models, but they are not known for good casting ability or durability, and although they catch fish, I prefer to opt for one of the models noted above.

Selecting Your Model:

Plug preference is a lot like food preferences in that one man's food is another man's poison. I've offered my ideas and opinions above, but that should not stop you from exploring the world of surface poppers, as I did. So, buy one plug and fish with it. How does it cast? Is it stable on the water? Is it easy to pop? How do the hook hangers, through wiring, and hooks stand up to saltwater gamefish? Also, consider that one popper might out-produce another in a given situation because of a variety of factors. Thus, it becomes important to explore which plugs work best in your backyard as well as which ones best fit your tackle and your style of fishing. In the end, after some experimentation, use the models, sizes, and colors that have a proven track record for you.

Summary:

1. Experiment with a variety of poppers and settle on those models, colors, and sizes that produce best for you.
2. Generally speaking, slosh standard poppers rather than work them quickly.
3. Pop strongly only when conditions demand that the angler grab the attention of preoccupied fish or when the surf is noisy.
4. Super Strike and Gibbs Polaris poppers can be used at night when long casts are needed, because they swim when retrieved slowly.
5. Pick your poison - wood or plastic.

6. White is a basic color found on all baitfish. It's a great place to start.
7. Bull style poppers make the most commotion and loudest sounds when popped.
8. Consider trying several of the many brands of "cottage brand" poppers. Most bait and tackle stores sell one or more of the locally produced brands.

Chapter 10
LURES THAT CATCH FISH: METAL LURES

"Tins":

Metal lures are often called "tins" because some are made with all tin and others are alloys of tin and other metals. Over time, anglers came around to calling them "tins," and soon everyone knew exactly what that meant. Many decades ago, anglers had a limited selection of metal lures to choose from, and if we go back, they also weren't chromed. As I pointed out earlier, anglers would scrub the tins in the beach sand to remove oxidation and induce a shiny surface.

Choices:

Today's anglers can select from an enormous variety of metal lures. There are the well-known and popular flat-sided models such as Kastmaster and Hopkins, as well as more precisely shaped metal lures; each with a different overall shape, some with keels, and some thick and others that are thin. There are also metal lures designed for long stemmed hooks and tubes. The tubes are available in almost every color, and the size ranges from fat, to medium, to thin in diameter. The available tube sizes make it easy to match a certain size tin with the right size tube, creating a balanced lure and a better presentation. A large diameter tube on a one-ounce tin isn't a proper balance, nor is a narrow tube on a three-ounce tin. In recent decades surf anglers have even adapted diamond jigs for the surf, including adding tubes to long hooks. Diamond jigs are especially useful in very rough water, when very long casts are called for, or when a stiff wind blows onshore.

Most commonly, tubes are used on metal lures when sand eels are the dominant bait. One style that's produced in my neck of the woods is the Spoon Jig, and I use it a lot in early spring while fishing in back bays, sounds, and harbors. The Spoon Jig is a narrow chromed piece of lead with a specific bend in it and with a narrow tube trailing behind. The bend in the metal creates swimming action and the tube wiggles back and forth too. I've found the double action to be very effective at times, and the spoon-like bend in the metal causes the lure to ride higher in the water, allowing me to use this lure in skinny water. Although I can provide no proof for the following opinion, it has evolved as a result of decades of fishing with metal lures with tubes. My opinion is that, although the metal jig does provide action to the tube, the fish actually pay little if any attention to the metal: rather focusing on the curved tube that imitates a sand eel. That may seem to be a rather unimportant conclusion, however, it tells me that I should not fuss over the style of metal as long as it allows me to present the tube properly. As an example, I go back to the Spoon Jig. I believe it is effective because it adds wiggle to the tube, and because I'm able to use it in very skinny water.

West End Tackle produces my favorite line of tins. Many decades ago a Long Island fishermen became famous because

West End Tackle's Charlie Graves tins are consistently effective and available in many shapes to match a variety of baitfish. (Zeno Hromin photo)

of the tins he designed. His name was Charlie Graves and his reputation, although enormous in his lifetime, has transcended the decades after his death. Ralph Votta acquired the molds for the Charlie Graves lures and has produced them ever since. Ralph is an outstanding beach fisherman and I'm envious of his ability to make a tin "sing." Over the years I've tried to pick Ralph's brain about fishing with "tins," and he's been kind enough to tutor me with some success. Some of my favorite Charlie Graves styles include the "J" series model numbers 1 to 8 (the larger the number the heavier the tin), the "D" series, the 4-ounce WS II, the pure tin Sand Flea, the RV series, the 2 ounce B1, and the 2 ounce High Glider. Each series has a different shape and has been designed to match specific bait (example: sand flea), or to run deep or high in the water column. The new D5S with a green tube became a staple for me during the recent fall run of sand eels.

Tubes:

Sand eels become very abundant along parts of the coast from time to time, and gamefish gobble them up readily. However, sometimes other fat-rich bait is also available and that presents an option for predators. Generally, predators will seek out the fat-rich bait like peanut bunker if it's abundant in preference to sand eels. On the other hand, when sand eels are the only abundant baitfish, predators home in on them, tide after tide, and tins with tubes become the hottest lures. If both sand eels and bunker are abundant, I'll usually work with bucktails most of the time.

Tubes can be added to any metal lure, but some tins are better matches to tubes than others. Diamond jigs, Teardrop tins, Spoon-Jig tins, and other thick model tins like the Charlie Graves "J" and "D" series are best. The weight of the tin to be used is determined by the size of the surf, much the way we select bucktail sizes. Although small sand eels may abound in calm backwaters in spring, fall-run sand eels usually attract more attention from predators because they are typically large (approximately 6 inches), and autumn's rough seas (up to 12 feet) make it easy for the fish to feed on sand eels.

Tins with tubes are extremely effective when the main forage is sand eels. (Zeno Hromin photo)

Presentations:

Just like bucktails, tins can be retrieved in a variety of ways, but slow and steady is often the best approach. Yes, there are days when a little jigging will grab the attention of a passing striper, and there are times when a periodic pause will snare fish too. Surf men who are experienced with tins also drag them through the sand and lift them periodically. Ralph has explained an interesting technique to me. He lays a tin on an offshore bar, drags it in the sand until it begins to fall along the inside slope of the bar, and then speeds up the retrieve. Ralph says that stripers cruising along on the inside edge of the offshore bar will see the sudden movement and attack the tin. However, the best all-around presentation is to keep the tins gliding and wiggling along within a foot or so of the bottom. On rough water days the angler needs to do nothing but retrieve the lure, because the heaving and crashing waves will do all the work for the angler.

Perhaps one of the most frustrating situations for anglers, regardless of the lure being used, is a crosswind. Crosswinds create a sweep in the surf that can push a lure into the wash almost as soon as it hits the water. Crosswinds also “grab” the line, creating a “sail” effect that pulls the lure along, often at the surface, resulting in a bad presentation.

Although we can’t stop the sweep, there are a few things an angler can do to get the lure down and keep it in the strike zone. First, use heavier tins in high seas and in crosswinds. Heavier tins will sink faster and thus minimize the ability of the wind to “grab’ the line. Once the waves exceed six feet and/or when the crosswinds exceed fifteen miles per hour, I use tins weighing between two and a half and four ounces. Remember the earlier discussion about having the right tackle to deal with surf conditions? Well, achieving proper presentations in big waves and crosswinds represents an excellent example of the need to match tackle to the existing conditions. A word to the wise, don’t be underpowered or you’ll be out of luck. Heavy tins will get down faster and you can also lower your rod tip close to the surface to minimize the effect of a strong crosswind.

Experienced beach fishermen often talk about allowing the tin to hit the sand from time to time. The idea is to let the tin bump

Heavy tins "grab" the water when big waves and winds interfere with surface presentations. (Zeno Hromin photo)

the bottom and raise a puff of sand creating the illusion of a baitfish being spooked out of the sand. Other advice from the experts includes letting a tin roll along the bottom in a sweeping sea while watching the line for a "jump" that signals the hit. I've used this approach in big waves and it is productive, but it takes discipline to overcome the urge to retrieve. Line watching is a useful tool in wavy and windy situations; helping anglers to know when to set a hook. I know that on more than one occasion my intense focus on the line while the wind whipped past my eyes, caused my eyes to tear so heavily I couldn't see the white caps let alone my line.

The Twitch:

Although low, steady, and slow is the best overall way to retrieve a tin, once in a while I'll snap my wrist upward creating a slight twitch at the lure end. Don't move the tin so much that you create an aggressive movement of the lure, rather create a small twitch. If there are any fish in the area, or if one is following your lure, the twitch often triggers the predator-prey response, leading to a hit.

Although others may disagree, my fifty-plus years of surf fishing has taught me that subtle moves are better than aggressive ones, most of the time. Typically, less is more. We are fortunate to have graphite rods and braided lines that allow us to confidently induce subtle movements in lures. With stretchy monofilament line, I was never quite sure whether or not the lure moved at the end of a cast. Did the lure twitch when I jigged or twitched? Or, did the line simply stretched with little or no lure movement? Thus, I tended to overcompensate for my concern about the stretch of monofilament by jigging too aggressively.

Pause:

Pausing once or twice during the retrieve is another subtle move that often triggers a hit. Any lure that suddenly sinks towards the bottom imitates dying fish, worms, or crustaceans. Wounded and dying baits are easier to catch, and the sinking motion often triggers predators to strike.

Too many anglers rarely or never give a thought to how different retrieves affect fish. Paying attention to the relationships between types of movement and fish responses when using bucktails, tins, and soft plastics can provide a great deal of insight into the difference between good and bad presentations. Also, remember that these lures can be worked at all water levels. Subtle twitches, pauses, snaps, brief accelerations, and rod angles all can potentially trigger a strike from fish that are in neutral or negative feeding modes. Although 90% of fish caught will be taken with the "standard" retrieve for that particular lure, advanced anglers use an arsenal of subtle movements to catch fish when they aren't feeding actively.

Summary:

1. The modern arsenal of tins includes a variety of sizes, weights, shapes, and actions. Each style has been designed to mimic different baits and applications.
2. Tins come with naked hooks, bucktail hair, feathers, and tubes. Adjust tail embellishments to the bait, sea conditions, weather, and size of the fish.
3. Presentations
    a. Basic: slow and steady.
    b. Advanced and subtle.
        1. The twitch
        2. The snap
        3. The pause
        4. Sudden accelerations and decelerations

Chapter 11 LURES THAT CATCH FISH: BIG SWIMMERS

Roll Call:

The roll call of basic designs for large swimmers is limited, although variations in size, color, and proportions seem limitless. Since large versions of plastic narrow Scandinavian style swimmers will be covered in the next chapter, that leaves three basic large swimmer designs: bottle plugs, darters, and metal-lipped swimmers. We'll also include large needle fish lures in this chapter, not so much because they are swimmers, and not so much because they are *always* large, rather because they are unique unto themselves and don't warrant a separate chapter, and because many surf anglers fish with the larger models at night and, when retrieved slowly, they swim.

From a somewhat limited vantage point that dates well back into the twentieth century, lure builders have tweaked these designs and morphed them into hybrids such as the bottle-darter.

Lure Designers:

More than any other style of lure in use today, the anglers who have developed, refined, and redesigned large swimmers are the most creative, precise, demanding, and artistic of the lure designers. In recent years, a new generation of lure designers, working mostly with wood, have burst upon the scene. These designers have hit on a number of successful designs too, and I admire their talents. But they are new to the angling scene, while the men who invented these lures and perfected them have been at it for decades. One aspect of lure design that all of them toiled over was to balance the lures so they would cast well and swim consistently. Success is as much a science as it is an art. Unfortunately and sadly, many of these pioneers are no longer with us, but happily some of the best artists are still designing, tweaking, and researching ways to make the lures perform even better.

My long-term friend Don Musso is an excellent case in point. Donnie is the founder of Super Strike Lures. While some designers stuck with unreliable wood as a base material, Don realized the advantages of plastic and set upon adapting his wooden lures to a plastic format. Was he successful? You bet he was! Super Strike continues to produce high-quality fish catching lures.

I believe it is important to note at least some of the giants who have toiled in pursuit of perfection, and upon whose backs we ride to angling glory. Jack "The Professor" Frech may get a lot of the credit for bringing bottle plugs and darters into general use among surf anglers, but his efforts would have fallen flat if it wasn't for the designers whose skills turned simple wood into magnificent tools for fishing. But Jack did create a variety of other wooden lures including poppers, metal-lipped swimmers, and jointed plugs too. Yet Jack never produced his designs for sale. His goal was to provide himself with an edge in competitive fishing against other talented anglers. Regardless, I salute them all: all the big plug guys from Frech, to Bob Pond to Don Musso.

The "Big Three" of big swimmers. Left to right: Bottle Plug, Darter, Metal Lip Swimmer. (Zeno Hromin photo)

Another important consideration for this chapter is tackle size. If you are a devotee of light tackle, I respect that if it makes you happy. However, if you want to fish with large swimmers, you'll need tackle that can handle the task. Please don't write to me to tell me how your light nine-footer casts three-ounce darters and bottle plugs, because I know better. An eleven-foot medium action rod is best. Not only are these lures heavy, but they also boast considerable wind resistance since they are fat and not thin: with the exception of needlefish. Stout surf tackle is needed to "power" these lures to a respectable distance off the beach. An eleven-foot medium power, medium action rod, such as the one repeatedly discussed in this book, but specifically described in chapters one and two, are the best matches for the job. True, my nine-foot GSB medium gets the job done, but not if there's a wind in my face. Large diameter spool reels and braided lines complete the picture of an outfit that will allow you to really cast and work large swimmers.

Bottle Plugs:

Bottle plugs are so-called because their overall shape resembles a bottle. They do not have either a metal or plastic lip, but the head of the plug is carved away to a curved slope. It's the curved surface that digs into the water and allows it to fall off to the sides, producing a wiggle. Bottle plugs imitate large prey items that struggle to swim. Although the action is regular and consistent, bottle plugs produce a distressed wiggle as opposed to a tighter wiggle more typical of a prey item in good health, and swimming normally.

Although these lures come in many sizes from about one-ounce to over three-ounces, the most commonly used sizes range from two and one-half ounces to more than three ounces. Super Strike's 2 ⅜ ounce Little Neck Deep Swimmer; in plastic, is a mainstay among devotees of bottle plugs. Gibbs, owning a long tradition of manufacturing large swimmers from wood, produces a variety of sizes, but perhaps this company's most popular size is the 3 ounce Casting Swimmer (aka Bottle Plug). Other old-time designs developed by Bob Hahn, included bottles in many sizes up to three and a half-ounces.

Fishing With The "Bottle:"

The following description presumes you have a rod and reel that can accomplish what I'm describing.

Cast the bottle plug as far as possible, lower the rod tip so that it is parallel with the surface of the water, and reel fast to first pick up slack line, and then to encourage the bottle to "dig." If you've done this properly, you'll feel tension on the line and your rod tip will throb as the plug wiggles back and forth. Just as these plugs offer considerable resistance to the air, so too do they resist the water. The drag on bottles is much greater than most first-timers expect. This completes phase one of the presentation: getting the plug to dig. If you fail to get the plug to dig, lower the tip of your rod and repeat the process. Do this as many times as needed until the bottle pulls and wiggles.

Phase two involves keeping the plug in gear, so to speak. Bottles are easiest to present and retrieve in moving water, such as a rip, but I have fished with them successfully in the ocean too. Generally, when the lure is fished in a rip, the current does the work of maintaining the lure's action once you've gotten it to dig. Sometimes, in strong rips, I've cast, made the plug dig, and then, because the current was strong, simply held on without reeling as the current swept the plug down-tide in an arc towards shore. Most hits come on the "swing."

Anglers need to work a lot harder when fishing in the ocean. Although on several occasions I have succeeded, let me say that I don't generally fish bottles in calm water, because they just don't seem to be all that effective when fish get long clear looks at the lure. Also, when the ocean is crazy, bottle plugs are very hard to control and do a lot of flopping even in the hands of an experienced skilled angler. On such days, I opt for a big heavy bucktail instead.

However, when the waves are in the three to five-foot range, bottles can be used successfully if the angler is on top of his or her game. What do I mean by this statement? Waves rise and fall; a process often referred to as heaving. When the "foot" of a wave touches bottom, it lifts and narrows. The net affect of this change in the wave is to push anything in front of the wave forward. At such times an angler needs to speed up the retrieve to maintain a throbbing action on the lure. This should be done at the first sign of a reduction in the pull of the water on the lure. Once the wave front passes, the lure is now on the back of the wave. Here, the water pulls down and back. Thus the drag increases and the angler should slow the retrieve and, at times, even stop the retrieve completely until the next wave front approaches. "Keeping in touch" with the lure, as experienced anglers say, is a key to the successful use of this lure in wavy surf. If an angler can't keep the lure swimming, it will flop like a piece of seaweed or other flotsam and not attract or trigger a strike. To top it off, every time an angler loses contact with the plug, it must be dug into the water again before resuming a normal retrieve. Although sustaining a proper presentation takes focus and concentration, the results can be worth the effort when large food such as bunker, herring, snapper blues, or various young of year fish are in the ocean trough.

Although some anglers are fussy about color, once again I am not. I will concede the importance of using yellow bottle plugs and darters at Montauk. In addition I will concede the point that some colors work better than others at certain locations because of the color of the bottom or seaweeds that cause bait to appear green, yellow, or reddish, for that matter. However, in most spots, "white is right!"

Darters:

Without belaboring the discussion about bottle plugs, let's move onto darters. Darters, unlike the arcing curved head of bottles, have straight, sloped heads, and it's the slope that creates the action. A flat surface is less efficient at holding water, so darters are less stable. The slightest disturbance in water flow can kick them off their motion causing them to roll over and come to the surface. As a result, they are more difficult to fish with than bottle plugs: especially in the ocean.

Darters are very effective at night, especially in currents. (Steve Kivlehan photo)

Fishing With The Darter:

Darters are at home in rips and these are the best venues for their use. Again, cast the lure out, lower the rod tip, and make several fast turns of the reel handle. Again, when the lure digs, water resistance increases and the lure begins to swim and dart. It is this irregular back and forth swinging or darting action that gives the lure its name. The darting action is in addition to a wiggle. It is a lot harder to stay in contact with a darter compared to a bottle plug, and as I've already mentioned, darters are more likely to lose balanced contact with the water. However, if an angler can develop some skill with the plug, the double action of wiggle and irregular darting action mimics a wounded prey, and there are times when this lure attracts more attention from gamefish than any other lure in your bag. It is worth developing a comfort zone with bottle plugs and darters.

Bottle-Darters:

A bottle-darter is a hybrid of a bottle plug and a darter. NorthBar Lures makes this lure in a variety of colors in two sizes: three as well as two and a half-ounces. The plugs are available in both wood and plastic. The concept of the lure involves combining the actions of both a bottle plug and a darter while achieving greater stability in the water when compared to the darter.

Cast the lure out, get it to dig, and retrieve the lure so that wiggle and darting action is maintained throughout the retrieve.

Metal Lipped Swimmers:

These large fat-bodied lures are niche lures. That is, they were designed for specific conditions and situations, and are not effective, day-in and day-out throughout the season, under a variety of physical conditions. What is a niche lure?

As mentioned, bottle plugs, darters, and bottle darters work best in moving water. Also, they are most effective when large baits are in the area. Finally, they can also be used in the ocean within a range of wave heights that permit continuous contact with the lures. Compare the use of big swimmers with bucktails or small narrow-bodied swimmers that can be used almost anywhere and consistently through the season, and the concept of niche lures quickly becomes solidified.

Metal-lipped swimmers are fat-bodied swimming plugs, typically made of wood, but some good ones are made from

Metal Lip swimmers are most effective in relatively calm water when fish feed on large baits. (Zeno Hromin photo)

plastic too. A bent piece of metal in the face of the lure is the lip, and it is this piece of metal that grabs and releases water off the sides as the lure pushes through the water, producing the wiggle and rolling action so familiar with fans of the metal-lip plug.

Unlike bottles, darters, and bottle-darters, metal-lipped swimmers work best in calm or relatively calm water. Metal lips may be used in a gentle swell as long as the angler is focused and maintains contact with the lure, especially when the lure is on the front side of the wave. In calm water, presentation is a snap.

Some metal lip swimmers have sloped heads. This design is intended to grab the water with the lip and the inclined head of the plug, so that the plug pushes deeper into the water. Although effective is some situations and preferred by some anglers, I prefer a darter, bottle plug, or bucktail if I want my lure to run deeper.

There are many brands of metal lip swimmers on the market today. Like other large plugs, many are produced in small quantities and sold for the local market. However, several of the better-known and readily available brands remain Danny Plugs (by Gibbs Lures in standard and Pro Series) and Atom Swimmers. Gibbs' Danny swimmer is made of wood and comes in three sizes: 1 ½ 2 ¼, and 3 ¼-inches. Atom's swimmers are made with compressed plastic foam, and also come in three sizes. The smallest is the Spin Atom, the middleweight is the Junior Atom, and the heavyweight is the Atom 40. The company also made a Reverse Atom 40 designed to be fished backwards. It has been said that the Reverse Atom had an action that mimicked the swimming of squid.

Historically, several terrific lines of metal lip swimmers were made but are no longer on the market. Don Musso produced several metal lip swimmers in wood that were favorite lures of mine. The Rattler was a slanted head swimmer in 6, 7 ¼, and 8 ¼-inch sizes. The Torpedo Swimmer with a round head also came in the same sizes as the Rattler. Bob Hahn also produced a line of metal lip swimmers that are highly regarded.

Another item of information that has more historical interest than it does modern relevance is the eel-skin plug, not because the plug doesn't catch fish anymore, rather because so few anglers take the time and trouble to rig them up. Basically, you take the hooks off a medium Danny or Atom Junior, and then you pull an eel-skin over the plug. Finally, reattach the belly hooks, but leave the rear treble off. Larger plugs were also used, but I think the medium models were most popular for this adaptation. These metal lip swimmers, fitted with eel-skins wiggle, waddle, and rock and roll seductively and the design has caught many trophy fish over the decades.

Tuning A Metal Lip Plug:

Although these plugs can be tuned to perform in different ways in response to different needs and conditions, it is wise to remember that expert lure makers have designed these plugs. Thus, I've always applied the idea of making careful, small adjustments in order not to undo the work of the artists.

The most common way to tune a metal plug is to bend the front eye up or down. When the eye is bent up, the lure will run deeper, while when the eye is bent down, the lure will ride closer to, or even at, the surface. I generally prefer metal lips to run at the surface, thus creating a big wake, and they also roll from side to side. Therefore, I usually bend the eye down. The

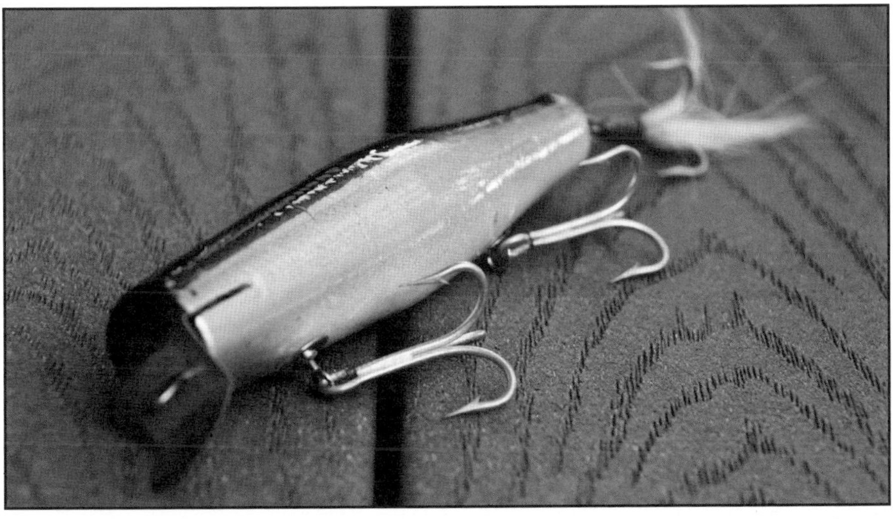

Bending the eye down makes the lure swim higher, while bending it up causes it to swim down. (Zeno Hromin photo)

only caveat that I can offer about bending the eye is to make sure the eye is straight and not crooked or bent off to one side, to ensure the best balance. Otherwise, bending the eye is a safe maneuver.

That isn't the case when it comes to bending the metal lip. I really try hard to stay away from manipulating the lip. Unfortunately, from time to time a fish will mangle it or tilt it off center, or manipulate a treble so that one prong grabs the metal and distorts its shape. Also, from time to time, I want to change the wiggle a bit, but I need to be careful because it's easy to distort the action and possibly never to be able to get the lip back to its original shape and action. Metal lips are bent twice. Once for the flat horizontal portion that goes into the body of the plug. A second portion, metal face, is pointing down at right angles to the face of the plug. The second bend is made up towards the first bend. Sometimes this bend is also a right angle bend, but other times the bend is roughly forty-five degrees. The lure maker selects the bend that produces a wiggle that is most compatible to the other qualities of the lure. For instance, is the face of the plug a straight, flat surface, or a rounded one? Or, is the dorsal surface of the plug sloped? How fat is the lure's body? Selecting the right piece of metal and bending it in a manner most advantageous to the plug is part of the lure designer's talent.

Some anglers also play with the action of these lures by changing the hooks or removing hooks. For instance, some surf rats will remove the rear treble and replace it with a few feathers or bucktail hairs tied around a thin metal shaft. Obviously, stainless steel is the best base for the rear teaser. Less weight in the rear of the plug equates to a larger and faster wiggle-wobble. An angler may also replace the treble hook with a single short-shank hook and sometimes add some feathers or hair to this hook. Some anglers even leave the rear of the plug bare.

Still other anglers will remove the hooks and upgrade to large treble hooks or stronger ones. Heavier trebles slow the action, while a change to lighter trebles speeds the wiggle up. Last reminder: be careful about bending the lip, and if you decide to bend it, don't be aggressive.

Teasers Ahoy!

Some devotees of metal lip plugs like to fish with a teaser at the front end of the leader. They claim it enhances the productivity of the plug. Although I don't use teasers often, who am I to argue, since these anglers have repeatedly proven their mettle on the beach?

Popping The Metal Lip:

This maneuver can only be done with a metal lip plug that swims at the surface. That need eliminates the use of sloped head metal lip plugs because they run deep. Also eliminated are some metal lip plugs that run a few inches below the surface. Although not in common use, some metal lip plugs sink: either because of added weights, or the use of dense wood, and these are also not appropriate for popping.

The concept of popping a metal lip plug is simple. The plug is retrieved in the usual slow manner so that it wiggles and rolls while throwing a wake to the sides. Every once it a while, perhaps two or three times during the retrieve, the angler pulls back on the rod. Do not snap the rod up and to the rear because that could result in the lure either diving deeper or sliding across the surface. The pull of the rod up and back is executed with a moderately forceful pull. The plug doesn't really pop, rather it sloshes ahead, spraying some water. The angler immediately returns to a normal retrieve. It takes a while to get the hang of this action, and different metal lip plugs will require more or less force on the pull back in order to get the right "slosh." Anglers who "live line" bunker from boats have a handle on why this works. A common practice in live lining is to pull back on the live bunker swimming at the surface when a striper is swimming underneath. The bunker will be nervous, and change direction often when it's being hunted. Should the bunker suddenly calm down, the angler may pull back, making the bunker slosh at the surface, and this action often re-energizes the striper's interest in the bunker.

The pop or slosh is intended to elicit a reaction strike from fish that are following the plug but have not attacked it. If you overdo the popping action, that is do it too often, you negate the positive triggering action because the metal lip swimmer becomes more like a popper and less like a swimmer. Two or three sloshes per retrieve are about right.

Summary:

1. Metal lip plugs are fat-bodied niche lures and are best used in calmer waters.
2. Metal lip plugs are made of either wood or plastic.
3. Metal lip plugs generally imitate large baits, but smaller metal lips are available and catch fish too.
4. The metal lip creates its action by grabbing the water and allowing water to slip off the sides of the metal, alternating from one side to the other.
5. Metal lip plugs seem to be most effective when they roll as well as wiggle.
6. Some metal lip plugs have blunt front ends, while others have rounded fronts with sloped dorsal surfaces.
7. Some anglers use a teaser ahead of the plug to enhance its appeal.
8. Metal lip plugs may be tuned in a variety of ways to make them swim differently. Bending the eye of the plug up or down causes the plug to ride higher or lower. Changing hook-sizes, or the number of hooks, alters the wiggle action.
9. Metal lip plugs may be draped with eel skins to enhance their appeal.
10. Be careful about bending the lip. The wrong move can destroy the plug's action.
11. Some metal lip plugs do not have a rear treble hook, but use a teaser end instead.

Chapter 12
LURES THAT CATCH FISH: SMALL SWIMMERS

Roll Call:

Although small versions of metal lip swimmers, bottle plugs, and darters are sold, for purposes of this discussion I will limit the discussion to hard plastic swimming plugs. Today's small hard plastic swimmers reflect a high level of technology that has gradually evolved and is used by lure designers and manufacturers to produce an array of very realistic plugs. The proof is found in the variety of models offered in bait and tackle stores, catalogs, and online. Today's products boast a high level of consistent quality, a diversity of swimming actions, and unbelievably realistic finishes.

Swimming action varies widely. Some plugs have tight wiggles, others more sweeping wiggles, and still others roll from side to side as they wiggle. As a result, anglers are the beneficiaries of abundant lure options that can be adapted to mimic many types of bait. It was only a few decades ago that there was a limited hard plastic arsenal on dealer shelves intended to meet the needs of freshwater anglers. Among the most popular lures in the early years were Rebels, Rapalas, and RedFins. The limited list is a thing of the past. In present time, any compilation of lures would be too long to list in this book because the roll call would take too much space. So, instead of trying to itemize and discuss these plugs comprehensively, I intend to discuss the ones I use regularly as well as others that are very popular but that I may not use. Throughout the discussion, remember that most of these designs originated for freshwater use and have been adapted to saltwater use. It's only during the last few decades that some manufacturers produced plugs intended for use in the salt chuck.

What Is A Small Swimmer:

Call them twitch baits, jerk baits, crank baits, Scandinavian style swimmers, or small hard plastic swimmers, they are intended to mimic the profiles and swimming motions of small fishes. Unfortunately, the vocabulary associated with these lures has become very muddled in recent years because there are so many types of lures and very few descriptors that seem to make sense. As a result, these above common category names are used more along regional lines than as national or global designations. So, although a thin hard plastic swimmer was once called a jerk bait because freshwater anglers reeled it in, jerked it, and then reeled it steady again, today the term jerk bait is also used for thin soft plastics that are fitted with a hook instead of a lead head and twitched during the retrieve. To make matters worse these soft plastics are sometimes called "fluke baits" or jerk shads.

In another case, I twitch a suspending Rapala Husky Jerk, although it can be cranked straight too. So, is the Husky Jerk considered a "jerk bait," "twitch bait, or "crank bait?" Beats me!

Small plastic swimmers are available in a variety of shapes and colors. (Zeno Hromin photo)

In the end, any hard plastic lure with a swimming lip falls into this category, from the Bomber A-Salt to the Big-O lure of yesteryear. I believe that the long thin styles are more popular in saltwater, while the fat bodied forms are very popular in freshwater, but not widely used in the salt chuck. However, in spite of the fact that all the models discussed in this chapter are longer than they are thick, each model has its own characteristics and each swims slightly differently than the others.

Rebels:

The trusty Rebel Floating Minnow and Jointed Minnow swimmers are no longer as popular as they were during the great weakfish run of the 1970s, and I'm not sure if it's a trendy kind of thing or that anglers believe other newer models are better. I must admit, I don't use Rebels much anymore either, but now that I think about it, maybe I'll put some of my old ones into service this spring.

The five-inch straight swimmer was a favorite of mine for many years, but the jointed model seemed to be even more popular in some quarters. I was never a big fan of jointed models because I felt the screw eyes that connected the front and back segments were the lure's weakest links. There were nights, however, when jointed models, retrieved in ultra-slow motion out-fished straight versions significantly. Although I still prefer the one-piece models, I try to keep an open mind.

Larger, seven-inch Rebels were very effective any place there was a modest current. Although it is true that some of today's plastic swimmers wobble and roll too much in a decent current, the big Rebel seemed to grab the water and wiggle consistently. I often cast the seven-inch Rebel down current in an inlet and simply held on, letting the plug wiggle and swing towards shore in the current.

Weighted models had a quick and intense market lifespan, as I recall. They were very popular during the 1970s weakfish run and again during the return of stripers in the 1990s after the moratorium of the 1980s. Rebel also made several models with a small lead weight fixed into the lip, and for a few years this was a hot plug for me. They haven't made this model for some time.

I was never a fan of big-lipped deep diving hard plastics that are so ubiquitous in freshwater, simply because I believe that if I have to get down deeper, I'd rather use a bucktail. Other anglers disagree with me on this and I understand the rationale when fishing in freshwater for large and small-mouth bass, walleyes, and pike, but in saltwater I believe there are better options for getting deep. I'll discuss those options in later chapters.

RedFins:

C09 RedFin:

Cotton Cordell's RedFins have been around a long, long time and are still popular in both freshwater and saltwater fishing. I still use these lures a lot. The RedFins are built in such a way that they are more buoyant than Rebels and Bombers. Cotton Cordell and the Pradco Lure Company that builds them today have made small changes to the plugs over the years. The company has varied the lure's wall thickness over time, changed the lure's hardware, and alternated between adding rattles and no rattles. These changes have altered the swimming action and the depth at which the lures swim when retrieved. Most brands of floating hard plastics swim a couple of inches to a foot below the surface. RedFins, on the other hand, ride higher or even at the surface, wobble more, creating a unique presentation that mimics baitfish behavior differently from Rebels, Bombers, and other brands.

For example, in years when small sand eels are very abundant in the spring, stripers feed slightly differently from one night to the next because the behavior of the sand eels changes frequently. Some nights the sand eels hunker into the sand at sunset and it takes stripers a while to root them out with their snouts and push them into the water column. On such nights, the sand eels leave the sand when disturbed, but try to return as fast as they can. In this scenario most of the sand eels are near the bottom or in mid-water. Hard plastics that swim well below the surface are best. However, on some nights, especially those with a bright moon, sand eels may voluntarily leave the sand and swim just under the surface. In this case, the skinny fish provide a clear profile against the moonlit sky, and stripers cruise beneath them. The stripers pick off sand eels that stand out against the shiny interface of sea and air. High riding four and five-inch RedFins are often the ticket on bright nights in spring. A suggestion: take a few moments to determine the water level with the greatest abundance of bait. Such knowledge will allow you to make important decisions about which lures are the best fit for the conditions and how to retrieve them.

C10 RedFin:

The Seven-inch RedFin has been a staple in my quiet water daytime bag for many decades. It is especially effective from mid summer to early fall, in water ten feet deep or less, and when spearing, snappers, or both are abundant. I especially like to use them when there's a slow current sweeping across a flat or when water moves off a flat and into deeper water. Stripers like to cruise across the sand and mud flats in estuaries from about mid-July to mid-September looking for scattered schools of spearing and snapper blues. In this hunting mode, they pick off unsuspecting baits as they roam over the flats. The C10 RedFin swims at the surface, wiggles and rolls leaving a wide wake behind, and models with rattles generate low frequency sounds that stripers and blues can sense from a considerable distance.

Redfins swim on the surface and catch fish throughout the season. (Steve McKenna photo)

Hits are often savage, but the hook-up ratio is rather low compared to other surface lures. The low hook-up ratio isn't a concern to me because the lure usually triggers more hits under these conditions compared to poppers and other surface swimmers in this pattern.

As previously indicated, Pradco Lures has produced RedFins with rattles in some years and without rattles in other years. However, I like the rattle effect so much I add my own BBs to the plug when the manufacturer doesn't. It's easy to do. Drill a 1/8th inch hole slightly above and behind the triple red-fin mark, add three or four BBs, and then seal with thick epoxy and let cure for twenty-four hours. Ordinarily, epoxy will flow into the hole, so I let the glue sit until just before it completely sets up, and then I add it to the top of the hole in the plug. In another approach, I plug the hole with cork, sand it flush, and apply a layer of epoxy on top. Two applications are sometimes needed.

Bombers:

Long A:

The Bomber Long A has been around for decades. I believe it to be a stable swimmer, reliable fish catcher, consistently durable, and a good match for a variety of east coast baits from sand eels to spearing to bunker. I use the five and a half-inch size mostly in spring, and the seven-inch size mostly in the fall. However, whether it is spring or fall, these lures are better used at night. I do catch some fish in daylight under specific sets of conditions, but the lure is, in my opinion, more productive at night. Unlike RedFins that generally swim on or slightly under the surface, Bombers tend to run two to eight-inches below the surface depending upon the speed of the retrieve and whether or not there's a significant current.

It is important to appreciate that as water conditions vary, bait swims at different levels in the water column and therefore it is the bait that dictates where stripers, blues, and weakfish will feed. Fish can feed near the bottom; in which case I prefer bucktails, within a foot of the surface; in which case I'll use Bombers and a few other models, or near the surface; and then

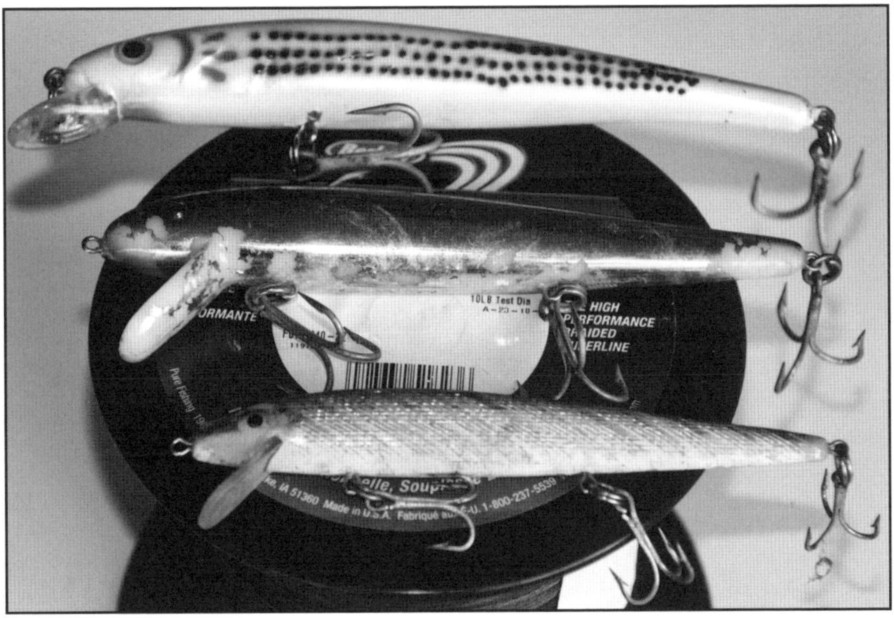

Small swimmers are more effective on big fish when the forage is small. (Zeno Hromin photo)

I switch to RedFins. Anglers tend to think about the phrase "match the hatch" in only one dimension, but I always try to understand as many dimensions of the phrase as possible. In this case, not only do I want to match the hatch for size and shape, but I also want a lure that fishes at a level in the water column where the fish are actively feeding. Although it is true that any of the three baits: RedFins, Bombers, or bucktails will catch some fish regardless of the feeding level of the fish, keying your lure to the right water depth will increase the catch.

Color:

Many anglers make a big fuss about lure colors, but as you already know, I don't fret about color. Many anglers simply can't fish at night without taking along a gaggle of "chicken scratch" hard plastic swimming plugs, including Bombers. Yes, I've caught lots of fish on "chicken scratch," but I've also caught plenty on many other colors. I think you get the point. I suppose it's fair to say that over the years I've used "flash" colors of Bombers frequently because those are the ones I have in my lure larder. For those of you who aren't familiar with the "flash" finished plugs, it is simply this. Mylar is positioned on the mid-line of the plug before the plastic is introduced. Once hard, the plastic is clear and the dorsal side of the plug is painted with a color (black, blue, green). The result is plug that reflects light on its sides and is dark on top. I like these patterns at night because I feel they "throw" some of the ambient light out to the sides, and the light may grab the attention of passing fish. The moral of the story is to pick whatever color you like, just fish it with conviction and make good presentations. Regardless of the color you choose, one thing is certain: if you don't believe in a lure, you won't catch many fish because your presentation will not be good!

Modifications:

I make modifications to the Long A Bomber in order to make it stronger and, I believe, a better fish catcher. Let me make it clear that it is not necessary to make these modifications in order to catch fish with the lure, but I often modify them nonetheless. I begin by removing the nose split ring (if the plug comes with one). The split ring will make the lure run deeper. Since I always use a terminal u-shaped snap and do not tie directly, removing the split ring does not restrict free-swinging action. Next, I remove the three trebles from the lure, upgrade to a number 1, 3X strong forged treble hook. I use Mustad 3561 ED and replace only the head and tail trebles leaving the mid-lure hanger empty. The number 1 hooks are heavier than the smaller hooks I've removed, but by replacing only two hooks with heavier hooks, balance is maintained and the overall weight remains virtually unchanged as well. As a result, I have a plug with stronger hooks, a plug that runs horizontally instead of slightly nose down, and has one less treble hook, improving safety for fish and angler alike, and the fish are easier to unhook.

Retrieves:

At night I retrieve Bombers the same way I retrieve the rest of the hard plastic swimmers on the market: steady, slow, and deliberate. By day I might periodically add a twitch, a pause, and a quick crank to the steady retrieve just to attract attention, but at night I do not. The best retrieve at night is usually so slow that it is agonizingly slow, and some anglers have trouble mustering the discipline to resist a faster retrieve. In my experience, the slower you can retrieve these lures, the better the chance you'll get a hit. To make the meaning of "slow" more accurate, let me offer this. If you aren't retrieving so slowly that you want to scream, then you are not retrieving slowly enough.

A-Salt:

I was instantly drawn to the A-Salt Bomber when it was introduced because I thought some of the lure's features were ideal for saltwater fishing. First, I like the slightly curved body. Second, I like that the lure was designed with hardware for saltwater use (unusual among hard plastic lures). Third, I like that there were only two trebles instead of the three sets found on Bomber's Long A models. Fourth, I like the extra heavy saltwater hooks on this lure. Then, when I fished with the lure, I discovered that A-Salt models have a knack of culling out the bigger fish in the area too.

Although I have had one or two A-Salt Bombers destroyed by big fish, generally they stand up to big fish and hard use, and I use them with confidence. Modifications are unnecessary and the lures come in a variety of colors including everyone's beloved "chicken scratch." So I'm confident anglers can find a few colors that instill them with confidence. The A-Salt model runs several inches below the surface but can be induced to run deeper with a faster retrieve. Keep this in mind and use a retrieve speed that best fits the depth of the water, where the bait is swimming, and whether or not there are bottom obstructions such as logs, rocks, and shell bars.

HellCats:

These lures are no longer in production and more than one angler might say "good riddance." Whopper-Stopper made two sizes of HellCats: five-inch and seven-inch models. Why did so many anglers make demeaning comments about the lures?

Perhaps the disdain resulted from a strong tendency of these lures to self-destruct under even modest pressure. Over the decades, I've had HellCats come back in pieces, plastic swim lips regularly came out, hooks constantly pulled out, and the two sides of the lure pulled apart at the glued center point. Then, why did anglers fish with them? The answer is simple: there were nights when HellCats were the only lures that would attract hits. As hard as that statement might be to believe, it's true. I always had one or two in my night bag just in case the fish became so fussy that all my others lures were rendered impotent.

But wait, the story gets better. HellCats caught more fish when retrieved very, very slowly. Interestingly, if an angler were to splash some light from a neck lamp on the lure during a slow retrieve, that angler would discover that the lure came in straight as an arrow-no swimming action. It was my lure of last resort, but I carried them and still do, for just the right occasion. If you find a few five-inch HellCats hidden in your basement or at a garage sale, buy them, clean them up, and carry them-just in case.

Some anglers believe color selections are vital, while others like me rarely fuss about it. (David Ryng photo)

Rapalas:

Rapalas are as old as the hills. Mr. Rapala designed the first few lures in this line in Finland many years ago, they were first sold in the U.S. in the 1930s, and his legacy lives on today. The original floating lure still catches tons of stripers, weakfish, and blues, but several more recent models are excellent fish-catchers too.

Perhaps one of the most popular models along the east coast is the X-Rap Shallow Shad model. Anglers like this plug because it runs a little deeper than Bombers and they are very strong. Since I do not fish with these lures, I asked anglers from local clubs about what Rapala models they like, and they indicated a preference for five and the half-inch SXR14 model in silver, spotted minnow, and glass ghost. The X-Rap also comes in a suspending model that some anglers use with success.

I use the suspending Husky Jerk Rapala in both fresh (smaller sizes) and saltwater (larger sizes) when I find that fish are feeding reluctantly in mid-water. In these situations, the ability to pause a lure and have it remain motionless, at a constant depth level, can trigger strikes from following fish. It's a niche lure for me and not my go-to hard plastic swimmer.

Yo-Zuri:

Yo-Zuri makes a number of minnow shaped swimmers, but I think a few are more generally used in saltwater than some others. In recent years, for example, the five-inch Mag Darter has become very popular along the striper coast. Anglers like the design that allows weight pellets to shift to the rear for longer casts, and then return to the mid-plug area during the retrieve in order to sustain a consistent swimming and darting action. Anglers also comment on the strength and durability of the Mag Darter. Favorite colors among the anglers I talked to were Ghost Blue Mackerel and Sardine. Anglers should be aware that Yo-Zuri lures are not inexpensive. The Mag Darter for example usually sells for about $15 although they are sometimes on sale for about $11.

Other minnow models, such as the Pins Minnow and Crystal Minnow, are popular among various groups of surf anglers, as is the new line of Sashimi Jerk Baits and minnows, but these are not fitted with saltwater hardware, so use them at your own risk. Yo-Zuri lures have a reputation as very good fish catchers, but I suggest you investigate the features of many models to help you select the lures that might serve your needs best under varying conditions.

Generic Copy Cats:

In the last two decades many new hard plastics swimmers have come on the market. Many come from established companies that invest a lot of money in design and testing. However, anglers should know that certain plastic injection molds are generic and are available and used around the world by a variety of companies. The shape is generic, but the lures are fitted with different hardware, packaging, stamped with different names, painted differently, and sold at discount prices under a wide variety of names. A close look will reveal that the array of lures all look the same but with cosmetic differences. That is not to say that these generic lures don't catch fish, because they do catch fish. However, anglers should be aware of this reality and purchase lures not by price, but rather from one's research and experience as well as the advice of well-seasoned anglers.

Summary:

1. All hard plastic swimmers are generally used in relatively calm quiet water, mostly at night, mostly in spring and summer, and mostly to match small baits such as sand eels, spearing, peanut bunker, and baby herring.
2. Different manufacturers' designs work best in specific situations according to the depth, action, and feeding mode of the fish.
3. The angler can't go wrong using well-known models from established companies such as those from Pradco (Rebels, RedFins, and Bombers), Storm Lures, Rapala's

original minnow and X-Rap, and others such as those from Yo-Zuri.

4. There are many models from a large number of manufacturers intended for freshwater use, and anglers can try to modify some of them for saltwater use.
5. Some anglers believe color selections are vital, while others like me rarely fuss about color.

Chapter 13
LURES THAT CATCH FISH: SOFT PLASTICS

A Sea Of Plenty:

Although soft plastic lures first appeared on the freshwater scene many decades ago, they weren't adapted to saltwater fishing until the late 1960s and 1970s. The first freshwater soft plastics I saw in the salt chuck were worms, but the catalog of soft plastic lures soon grew to include crayfish, lizards, curly tail worms, eels, and fish-like plastics hooked onto lead jig heads. Eventually, angler enthusiasm for soft plastic lures, combined with advances in the technology used to produce them, ushered in an era of complex and life-like imitations of small fish. Today, there are so many soft plastic designs offered by so many companies that it is impossible to cover them all. Furthermore, each year new colors come and go, as do slightly changed shapes, intended to keep freshwater bass anglers on their toes. The scent phenomenon has really taken hold in fresh water but has had little effect, in my opinion, on saltwater fishing for gamefish. From a humble beginning, today's soft plastics take up lots of wall space in bait and tackle shops and many pages in catalogs, too. The bulk of the soft plastics continue to be designed and produced for freshwater use, but there are a number of styles that have gained wide acceptance in the salt chuck.

The 1970s Weakfish Run:

I don't remember soft plastics being used in saltwater until the great weakfish run that lasted from the late 1960s into the early 1980s. Whereas previously bucktails and natural baits, such as sandworms and squid, were the mainstays of weakfish anglers, all of a sudden there were Mann's Jellyworms, Salty Dog Shrimp, and Touts. Sure enough we all started fishing with them and caught fish too. Little did we know at the time how diverse our selections would become in the 1990s.

Modern production methods and new types of materials have broadened the scope of soft plastic lure designs. (David Ryng photo)

Modern Choices:

Surf fishermen use lots of soft plastic lures, although they do have disadvantages. More about that in a bit. Right now, let me run down some of the more popular and widely used soft plastic lures in saltwater, including thin baitfish imitations, curly tails, jerk shad (fluke) variations, soft paddle tails, and swim baits. Many of today's models boast life-like colors, realism, and balance beyond anything anyone could have imagined in the late 1950s. In this chapter we'll take a look at each style and discuss how and why the design works, along with the best presentations to use for consistent success. Right now let's deal with the disadvantages.

Problems With Soft Plastic Lures:

As we've already begun to appreciate from previous chapters, there are problems and limitations with all styles of lures. Even my beloved bucktails are limiting. For instance, because they are made with lead, bucktails are very difficult to use in very shallow water, not only because of the limits of shallow water, but also because of the typical need for slow retrieves. In a second example, HellCats self-destruct, but there are still times when I'm glad to find one in my bag. Okay, all lures have positive and negative aspects.

By the nature of their composition, soft plastic lures lack durability. Most saltwater fish, whether they have teeth or not, will destroy them in short order. Of course that means the angler will need to retie or change lures frequently, and that takes time away from fishing. Softness also means anglers need to carry a bagful of bodies and although many soft plastics are not very expensive, the cost still adds up. There's simply no way to avoid these disadvantages.

Some soft plastics, such as swim baits, come with factory fitted hooks. Typically, they are not forged hooks, but wire hooks. True, the hooks are often of good quality, but they are still wire and not forged. Wire hooks are much easier to straighten and they corrode quicker too.

Soft plastic lures tend to have a poor weight-to-body surface ratio. That means many of them offer lots of wind resistance without a lot of weight, and casting distance suffers. If fish are feeding far off the beach, soft plastics cannot reach them no matter how hard an angler tries.

Although there are some soft plastics with large profile designs, most soft plastic lures are copies of small baits, and that limits their use. Small lures have poor weight to body surface ratios, even worse than bigger models, reducing casting distance even further.

Finally, I have found that these lures are basically one-dimensional, and only one presentation catches fish consistently. Some may be used in several ways, but most fit a specific presentation slot that severely limits the effectiveness of the lures. On the other hand, I can use bucktails in dozens of presentations and that's why I tend to use bucktails over soft plastics. In my private world, I use soft plastic lures most often in early and mid spring when three and four-inch baits such as sand eels dominate. In my experience, water temperature affects the productivity of soft plastics. When the water is cold, small soft plastic lures such as slender paddle-tail styles often out-fish tins and bucktails.

One retrieve that seems to be consistently effective involves casting the lure out and retrieving it straight with a moderate speed. If the retrieve is too slow, the tail either doesn't move much or not at all. If the retrieve is too fast, on the other hand, the lures tend to become unstable and may even spin. If the lures are jigged they become unstable and dart around in a very unnatural way that I've never found induces consistent strikes.

Saltwater Applications:

Little by little over the years, more and more soft plastic lures appeared on the market intended for saltwater use. Although worms continue to be popular among weakfish anglers, their popularity never really caught on among striper fishermen in most locales, probably because of limited casting capabilities. In addition, although straight-body "Jerk Shad" or "Fluke" styles are used among a dedicated group of surf fishermen who ply quiet waters during deep-night tides, their use in my experience also remains limited. For example, some anglers use a Fin-S, Bass Assassin, or similar form on a hook without a lead head, and cast these at night when stripers chase spearing against the shoreline and when long casts are not an issue.

In spite of a multitude of designs, however, of all the designs on the markets I believe two styles are more popular than the others: swim baits and long thinner paddle tail lures.

Popular Designs:

Swim Baits:

There is no doubt that the popularity of swim baits is enormous and growing. That's because they are relatively inexpensive, widely available, and require little skill to use. As stated before, an angler needs only to cast them out and retrieve steadily

Large, deep-bodied, paddle tail soft plastics are excellent when bunker, peanut bunker, and herring are abundant. (Zeno Hromin photo)

without jigging, and at a moderate speed. The lures require no finesse to catch fish. That's good news, but that doesn't diminish the reality that a bucktail and porkrind in the hands of an experienced angler will catch many more fish. In the end, lure selection is about experience, skill, comfort, and expectation.

I believe the Storm Wild-Eye swim bait was the first of the style to gain popularity along the east coast. However fishing, as in other industries and endeavors, is a copycat business. Soon other styles appeared. Tsunami, for example, began producing swim baits in a wide variety of colors and sizes from one-inch to seven-inches. The company tried to address one of the shortcomings of the Storm Wild-Eye (soft and easily ripped), by using a plastic formula that was a little firmer when it gelled. Indeed Tsunami Swim Shads are more durable, but with a slower tail action. There's always a compromise to be made when designing lures. I know of a small group of anglers that prefer the Tsunami models in tidal current since the moving water will induce more tail action. Storm's version, on the other hand, maintains excellent tail action in water without any current at all.

It has been my experience that swim baits perform best in water without a lot of wave action or turbulence. Turbulence, in the form of eddies and waves, tends to make swim baits roll, and renders a consistent presentation more difficult. In quiet water, however, the realism of their appearance and subtle swimming action can be an advantage since fish often become a lot more wary in calm water. Because the lures look so real, I'll use them in the ocean in a modest sea, towards the end of a tide, when the fish are well fed and begin to feed more slowly and cautiously. Often at this stage of a feeding period other lures such as tins, surface lures, and even bucktails are ignored, but an angler can often pick away on fish using swim baits. I usually use bunker or pearl colored models.

Paddle Tail Styles:

I was introduced to my first paddle tail soft plastic lures in the 1990s when more than one friend told me about Queen Cocohoe Minnows. The brand is still around and still catches fish. It's a four-inch soft plastic body that is threaded on a lead head with the hook exiting mid-body on the dorsal surface. I prefer the triangle and ball shaped lead heads in three-quarter and one-ounce sizes. In those days we used chartreuse green, pearl, and chartreuse with a red tail most of the time. I've found after experimenting that pearl and chartreuse produce more consistently than other colors.

Once I was introduced to the Cocohoe brand I began to notice generic shad bodies in all the tackle stores and catalogues too. Although some were sold in pre-packaged bags, most were found piled up in buckets and selling for a given number for a dollar or two. Again, these were bodies to be used on lead heads. We all bought them and used them and we caught lots of fish, too.

Then on a cold March day I went fishing in Rich Lazar's boat looking for early schoolies in the back of Manhasset Bay. Rich and his son Marc out-fished my Cocohoe minnows: maybe three to one. They were using a new paddle tail with a similar shape to the Cocohoe, but softer. The softer body was more pliable, allowing Rich and Marc to get good action out of the tail at very slow speeds. These were Samurai Shads from Yum. I bought bags of these and still use them today in the early season. I must admit, Samurai Shads aren't very durable, but they catch fish when other paddle tails don't.

There are dozens and dozens of paddle tail designs out there and although I haven't fished with all of them, I'm sure they all catch fish under the right conditions. New ones come and go so quickly that it's hard to keep track of the changing scene. However, there is one new design whose popularity skyrocketed in the fall of 2010 when large sand eels dominated along east coasts ocean beaches for several months. The company, Vision, took the long and thin concept to an extreme to imitate sand eels. They combined some hi-tech production techniques to produce Sand Eels and Surf Eels that are very realistic and, thanks to a paddle tail, squirm around like a sand eel. They don't cast well and although I tried, I was unable to cast them beyond the "lip" or curl in

New realistic sand eel imitations have become extremely popular in recent years. (Zeno Hromin photo)

rough water. However, anglers who use them often point out that these lures work best in quiet water at night, and as a result, they have gained great popularity among dedicated surf rats.

Curly Tails:

Mister Twister was one of the first big companies to make curly tail soft plastic lures. Today, curly tails come in sizes from the one-inch Teenie-Tail from Mister Twister to the giant six-inch Mogambo Curly tail from Kalin. These soft bodies are used on lead heads and as embellishments for bucktails. Although widely popular, I don't use them often in saltwater although I use smaller models frequently in freshwater. Many beach fishermen use three, four, and five-inch curly tails as add-ons for bucktails and they work. However, I'm convinced after decades of experimentation that the proper length and style of pork rinds on bucktails will out-fish curly tails most of the time. There is no ultimate "Platonian" way. That is, unlike a point of view put forth in Plato's Republic, there are many ways to approach surf fishing. I applaud them all if they represent the best approach to someone. Being comfortable with an approach is a key to success, but we should never turn our backs to new things and new techniques simply because we are satisfied with our production.

I made a vow years ago to never be satisfied with the status quo and, thanks to this commitment, I've been able to expand my fishing horizons beyond prior comfort levels, and I continue to embrace new ideas every year. I add to my bag of tricks those lures and techniques that are effective, but only after prolonged experimentation. I also reject those that fail or aren't as good as others. What I attempt to share in my articles, books, and seminars are those techniques and experiences that have proven credibility and work consistently. It's up to each angler to decide which of my ideas and suggestions can be wedded to their own style and habits.

Summary:

1. Soft plastic lure bodies were first developed for freshwater bass anglers and didn't gain wide use in the salt chuck until the 1970s weakfish run.
2. Swim baits are produced by many companies and are extremely popular among beach anglers.
3. Paddle tail styles are diverse in shape, color, and company of origin, but catch lots of fish when forage is small.
4. New realistic looking designs are sweeping across the surf crowd. One of the most recent, Vision's Sand Eel burst onto the scene coincidental to an abundance of large sand eels in the ocean surf.
5. Soft plastic lures have limitations including limited casting distance, a lack of durability, and they lack retrieve options.

Chapter 14
READING THE BEACH AND WATER

Venues:

Unfortunately, there are no maps available to direct an angler to specific sections of the beachfront that are likely to produce fish. That's where learning to "read the beach" comes into play. As with all aspects of surf fishing, it is a necessary skill that is acquired over time while ascending the learning curve. The value of learning how to read water and structure is found in the relationship between bait, fish, and structure. Indeed, the elements of bait, structure, and presentation are found at the heart of my fishing philosophy. That is, find and identify the bait, find and identify the structure, and then make precise repetitive lure presentations.

Why does this approach pay off so often? The sea and its various subdivisions aren't like land ecosystems. Land environments include grasslands, forests, rocky crags, caves, mixed foliage, layered rocks, and other structures in abundance. In the sea, on the other hand, places to hide are generally sparse. True, coral reefs, wrecks, and seamounts are stunning exceptions, but these are rare and scattered. The truth is that in temperate near-shore areas, dramatic structures tend to be limited. That's both good news and bad news. The bad news is that usable structure can be more difficult to find than on land, while the good news is that fewer structures means bait and gamefish have fewer structures for hiding and ambush, and that means if anglers find structure the chances of catching fish increases sharply.

Structure:

I use the word structure more loosely than hunters might, and freshwater anglers too, because with so little structure along most beaches even the subtlest of changes can attract and hold bait and fish. Therefore, we don't need a giant fallen tree, an old river channel, or an underwater mountain to find feeding fish. Often a drop of a few inches in the bottom is enough to create both a hiding place and feeding opportunity. In that sense then, I also include offbeat water movements that are generated by weather, waves, and bottom contours as structure, too. These water movements represent differences in water speed or direction of flow that attract living things. It's the equivalent of what trout fishermen call a "seam" in a stream: a linear difference in the movement of water. So, if I see an eddy created by wave action form along the beach, I immediately cast into it because I know the turbulence in the eddy tends to disable bait and offer gamefish a feeding advantage.

It is also valuable to consider that different bodies of water have different structural components. Each type of water body has unique characteristics including the type of structure, its permanence or lack there of, and its usefulness to the angler. Ocean sand beaches are the most ephemeral because big waves, small sand grains, wind driven sweeps, and erosion all conspire to move huge volumes of sand from one place to another in a very short time. That's why I assay the ocean beaches at the start of the fall run, but I know full well that any cuts, bars, points, or holes I find may no longer be there after the first nor'easter. On the other hand, I expect few changes in back bay areas because the effects of weather, waves, and currents are much less dramatic. Finally, I expect some changes in more open estuaries (sounds) because they are long enough and wide enough for big waves to form from storms, and the resulting waves change structure. Even in a sound such as Long Island Sound, some areas are more affected by waves, currents, and storms than others. Those areas dominated by sand tend to change quite a bit, while those with rocks and pebbles change little if at all. We'll take a detailed look at structure in these three locales.

Ocean:

Let's begin with ocean beach structure. Here's what I do and how I interpret what I see. For me, the beach structure zone extends from the offshore bar to the sand under my feet. The zone has three parts: the offshore bar zone, the trough, and the beachfront. Ideally, I like the offshore bar to be located about seventy-five to one hundred yards off the beach. If the bar is significantly closer than seventy-five yards the trough will tend to be shallow, while a bar located more than one hundred yards off the beach tends to not interact with the close-in surf zone. When the offshore bar is too far out, the bar tends to be more uniform, have few if any cuts, and any turbulence created on the bar by waves moving over it cannot be accessed by shore anglers. When the bar is located at the right distance, the trough will be deeper than five feet at low water, fish will tend to move between the bar and the beachfront more often, turbulence near the bar with interact with water in the trough, and the bar will tend to knock down powerful waves that would otherwise dirty the fishing zone. Since the distance from the bar to the beach is a short fetch, waves don't have time to reacquire their original force, and that means even storm waves will have lesser effects on the beachfront.

White water produced over bars reveals the shallow zones while darker areas are deeper. (Zeno Hromin photo)

How can an angler discern these structural components? The answer takes us back to the focus of this chapter: by reading the water. We read the water with our eyes and use knowledge about shallow water environments. Here's what happens. Waves tend to "feel" bottom in shallow water and, as a result, become taller and steeper until the structure of the wave can no longer support the mass of water in the wave, and it falls forward creating white water. We usually call such waves "breakers." Thus, where we see white water, we have shallow water, and where we don't see white water we have deeper water. The deeper the water, the darker the color; which allows us to estimate comparative water depths. Of course this presumes we have waves. It can be almost impossible to read certain beach structure on calm days by using wave action. The only option on calm days is to use polarized sunglasses and try to find sandy colored and deep blue-green areas. Obviously, sandy areas are shallower, while dark blue-green areas are deeper.

The offshore bar can either be a solid crest of sand that runs parallel to the beach, or it may be punctuated with cuts. A cut is a place where surging water creates a deeper opening between the trough and the ocean beyond the bar. Bars with cuts are preferable to continuous bars because the cuts represent places where baitfish can easily move from the ocean into the trough and vice versa. Once in the trough, gamefish find the bait and anglers can reach this feeding zone with lures.

Furthermore, during days with big waves that crash over the bar and into the trough, water builds in the trough with each wave creating a difference in sea level between the ocean and the trough. The extra water in the trough cannot run back out over the bar because new waves keep crashing across the bar and push more water into the trough. The only option available to equalize the water depth between trough and ocean is for the extra water in the trough to rush through a nearby cut and into the ocean. Thus, currents are created in the trough and around the cuts. Often water in the trough will move towards the cut from both sides of the cut. These currents will meet in front of the cut and turbulence will be created. Large eddies with white water turbulence will appear and disappear here, again and again. The turbulent water becomes a trap for baitfish that struggle to swim against the currents. Gamefish, on the other hand, have no such trouble with turbulent or even violent water for that matter, and they swim through these eddies to feed on the baitfish trapped helplessly within them. Turbulent eddies become magnets for me, and when I spot these confluences of water in front of cuts I rush to fish them.

Structure can also exist along the beachfront. This close-in zone can be straight, dotted with periodic coves, or scalloped, and the face of the beach can range from flat to severely sloped. Regardless of the beachfront irregularities, I prefer steep sloped beaches because it usually means the trough in front of the beach face is deep. I also look for small indentations along the shoreline where bait can accumulate as well as points of sand jutting out into the trough. Each irregularity represents an edge, and edges are places where bait attempts to hide and gamefish lurk as they seek feeding opportunities. Always think in terms of edges, whether you fish the ocean, back bays, or sounds. I cannot overstate the importance of edges, even small ones, because edges are fishy places. Try to find spots with as many irregularities of bottom and water movement as possible. If a number of irregular components are clustered together, it is likely that an angler will catch fish.

Points of sand that jut into the trough can improve fishing dramatically even when the point is small and unimpressive. If a point reaches out into the trough (becomes a bar) for some distance, then the productivity of the point will increase sharply. Improved fishing results because the underwater bar will have an edge on either side. The edges collect bait, while the waves flowing over the point bar will tend to accelerate. Why acceleration occurs can be a bit tricky to understand. Here's what happens. First, the level of the water on both sides of the underwater point, and in front of it must be the same. Second, as a slow moving volume of water is forced onto the underwater point from one side, that same volume of water needs to be transferred to the other side of the point and dumped into the deeper water. Third, as the water moves across the bar there's only one way for a given volume to move from deep water on one side to deep water on the other side without creating a depressed water level over the bar, and that's if the water speeds up while over the bar. Consider a stream. In the deeper parts of the stream the water moves quite calmly, but as the water approaches a shallow area it speeds up creating "rapids" so that the same volume of water can move through a given length of the stream. Some of these underwater points are "C" shaped due to the push of water from currents in the trough, over the bar, and back into deeper water. The "C" shape provides anglers with an abundance of reachable edges on the inside and outside of the comma shaped bar.

Thus, the keys to reading ocean beaches are white water, dark water, sandy colored bottom, deep blue-green bottom areas, and how water moves over bars and through troughs.

Back Bays:

Back bay areas are often neglected by anglers because they are shallow and far from the ocean. However, the deep recesses of bays and harbors tend to be littered with channels, creeks, drains, complex marshy shorelines, and very irregular rocky or sandy areas. These structures tend to be stable and many, such

Back bay and harbors are usually calm without white water areas, but shell bars, submerged boulders, and dock pilings are excellent structures. (Zeno Hromin photo)

as creeks and channels, also boast currents as the tide rises and falls.

Finding bait in backwater areas is much easier than in the frequently violent ocean expanse, and should be an angler's first priority. I fish around bait even when the bait isn't located near the best structure, but I do prefer bait shoals closer to structure. Typically, these structures are productive in association with very specific tidal windows. That is, some places like drains and creeks tend to produce on the outgoing tide, while flats tend to be most productive on incoming water.

Although large tidal ranges are sometimes intimidating to some anglers, I'd suggest you take a second look at the topic. Large tidal ranges can be a force for good or bad, depending upon your point of view. Although it is true that where tidal ranges are large in back bay areas certain bottom structures may be high and dry at times, it is also true that these same areas represent new feeding areas for gamefish as the tide turns and floods the structures.

Inlets:

Inlets offer at least one advantage over ocean beaches and backwater shorelines because, except for brief slack water intervals between tides, there is always current, and where there is current there are fish.

Many inlets also sport high rock jetties on their flanks to reduce erosion from storms. Rock piles provide homes for crabs, lobsters, small fish such as blackfish and gobies, and eels too. Gamefish often hunt where the rocks meet the sand. Jetty jockeys, surf anglers who fish atop rock piles, are a separate breed of cat. Their rods and reels are usually different, their outerwear selected specifically for the rocks, and their outings are often more adventurous. It may not be pure surf fishing, but it's a style that has its devoted fans. Many of us fish close to jetties from the sand where dead-end pockets along the sides of the jetties collect bait that are easy pickings for gamefish.

Sounds:

Sounds are big bodies of water that experience the effects of big waves during windstorms. These bodies of water also tend to be dotted with pronounced shoreline structures such as long points, boulder clusters, and dramatic coves. Typically, many creeks and rivers empty into Sounds on the ebb tide, dumping copious amounts of bait into the larger estuary, especially during bait migration periods.

Points of land are important because water is stacked up on the up-tide side of the structure and when this water escapes around the tip of the point it accelerates creating strong rips, and rips are excellent feeding zones for gamefish. Clusters of giant boulders and scattered shell bars, commonly found scattered around points and close to shorelines, also represent hiding and feeding stations for bait. As a result, gamefish routinely patrol these scattered structures.

Most sounds are replete with flats that typically make up the bottom in large coves. These flats are usually composed of sand, but more sheltered coves may also contain mud and/or shell bars. Mud flats are rich in worms, crabs, burrowing invertebrates, grass shrimp, mantis shrimp, and small fish, providing food for gamefish throughout the season. Stripers are often found feeding casually on flats. Usually, they are spread out, and in a spooky mood. Sandy flats, on the other hand, tend to produce best in spring when sand eels are abundant, and again in the fall when shoals of migrating baitfish cross the flats as they attempt to escape to the ocean. Sandy flats also stand up better to stormy weather compared to mud flats that are easily muddied.

Sounds are usually deeper than bays because they are so large. Deeper and shallower zones create microhabitats that result in a greater variety of bait types and often a larger biomass is supported in sounds. The shore topography of many sounds is dotted with large shallow recesses called harbors. Harbors are very productive areas, serving as nursery grounds for invertebrates, baitfish, and some gamefish. Therefore, at certain times of the year, especially from late summer into mid autumn, larger predators enter harbors from deeper water to feed on massive schools of bait. Many savvy surf rats gravitate to the shores of these harbors during prime months. Unfortunately, many harbors, similar to back-bay areas, are well developed and private property dominates these shores making access difficult. Still, there are enough town, county, and village parks to provide at least some access, while other shorelines provide limited nondescript access adjacent to street parking.

Sounds are big compared to inlets and bays. Therefore, similar to ocean beaches fish are able to retreat far off the beach in search of food. As a result, just like oceanfront, there are fewer productive days along sound beaches compared to bays and harbors because beach-bound anglers can only access a narrow zone of water. However, also similar to ocean beaches,

Sounds are large estuaries with subtle structures that are best read at low tides.

the potential exists during migration periods for more bait and more gamefish to accumulate along sound beaches compared to inlets and back-bay areas, providing occasional tides with phenomenal fishing.

Summary:

1. There are four main beach types: back-bays and harbors, inlets, sounds, and ocean beaches.
2. Ocean beach structure is very temporary. It comes and goes with every storm.
3. It is important that anglers learn to "read the water."
4. The best ocean structure includes an offshore bar (out approximately 75 yards), cuts in the bar, steep beach faces, and a deep trough.
5. Waves create the most important water currents in the ocean.
6. Back bays and harbors are shallow confined feeding zones and nursery grounds. Currents are created by tidal flow and not wave action.
7. Back-bays and harbors tend to sequester bait, producing periods of intense action.
8. Inlets feature a more or less constant current flow created by tidal action that moves bait and provides feeding opportunities for predators.
9. Sounds are large estuaries that feature more stable structure than ocean beaches, but where baitfish and gamefish movements more resemble ocean beaches.

Chapter 15
FIGHTING & LANDING FISH

Neglected Aspect:

When I speak with or tutor surf anglers, I get the impression that many of them believe fighting and landing fish does not deserve a lot of consideration. When asked about how they go about this part of fishing they simple say, "I just reel them in." Then, they look at me and seem to be thinking: *"Why are you asking me about that?"* Obviously, they think I've just arrived from another planet. However, in my experience, fighting and landing fish are some of the most neglected skills related to angling. As I watch people around me, generally it is done poorly. As with all things in fishing, exactly how we do something is a reflection of who you are and what you want. However, once again let me point out that since this is my book, I'll hop on my soapbox and let it all hang out.

Some anglers seem to want to hang on, rather than fight a fish. I find this to be obtuse since the hit and the fight are a large portion of the enjoyment of the sport. I stick them, I fish a tight drag, and I make the fish work. If they fall asleep, I wake them up.

A Memory:

Several years ago I was fortunate enough to get in on a run of fish during the fall. Unfortunately, only one large structure developed in the area and so all the bait, fish, and anglers were forced into a limited space. Now normally, on a beach with repeating structures, I walk until I run out of people before I fish. I'm not antisocial, but I become frustrated by anglers with the wrong equipment, who can't control their equipment, whose casting is all over the map, who kill fish indiscriminately, and have no compunction about mugging me if I should hook and land a nice fish. I don't go fishing looking for aggravation and frustration, rather I fish for fun, excitement, and the company of skillful peers. I don't want to argue so, when I can, I walk away.

Anyway, there were no fish anywhere else and I was forced into the crowd. Keep in mind that this was ocean water, often with big waves, and many of the fish were sizable. Here comes a fellow with a seven-foot rod and reel combo. He can't throw the right lures, he can't power the lure into the wind, and he can't reach the fish. Unfortunately, he didn't figure that out, so he stood firm, fumbling to catch a fish, his errant casts picked up the lines of other anglers, and he took a space away from someone who was equipped for the task.

In a second memory, a fellow was fishing next to me. His equipment was okay, but he should have put a bigger reel on his ten-foot rod. He skills were poor and this was manifested in poor casting and worse presentations, and while he caught nothing others around him picked away. However, just like the blind squirrel that manages to find an acorn in spite of his infirmity, this guy hooks up to a fish of about twenty pounds. His drag was set far too loose: probably because he didn't trust the knot he'd tied, and the fish ran helter-skelter back and forth as well as toward and then off the beach. Anglers were courteous and stopped fishing as the fellow's fish ran past them in one direction and back again. It took forever for this guy to land the fish and he inconvenienced dozens of anglers. Of course, the fish was exhausted and he kept it. Do you notice a trend in these stories? However, had he wanted to release it, I doubt strongly whether that fish was releasable. He didn't behave like a sportsman because he didn't demonstrate respect for other anglers or the fish he was fighting. Furthermore, this angler failed to understand a very important principle about fighting fish. That is, *the longer the battle, the more likely a hooked fish will get free.* So, ironically, the angler chose an approach that could have worked against him. I don't offer this story to exorcise my anger about the situation, rather as a cautionary tale to reinforce my earlier point that fighting and landing fish is an important skill set that needs to be learned and practiced if an angler wants to be considered to be a genuine surf fisherman. The same skills are also necessary in order to be a good steward of the sea.

Tackle First:

It is difficult and perhaps impossible for poor tackle, weak knots, bad line, and dull hooks to assist an angler during the processes of hooking up, battling, and landing fish. So, it all starts with the right stuff. As I've already pointed out, an improved clinch knot when tied properly is a very strong knot, and is very easy to tie. I urge anglers to practice tying this knot, and to get used to what a good knot looks like. With practice, you will gain confidence in tying and using the knot. Test your knots. Grab the leader in one hand and the running line in the other (about two or three feet apart) and then pull the lines in opposite directions. Put a little snap into that pull. If the knot is weak, the knot will break or slip. If it doesn't, use the knot with confidence. Make sure your tackle is up to the task. Also remember that big water demands relatively big tackle. Finally use a file to sharpen your hooks to a needlepoint in order to achieve better hookups.

Hooking:

When the fish strikes, use the length of your rod and your upper body to make a sharp backward thrust: that is, a strong

Using correct tackle and setting a proper drag conserves fish, and allows the angler to maintain control of the fighting fish. (Zeno Hromin photo)

movement away from the water. If your line and terminal knot are in good shape, there's no need to worry. A solid thrust is needed in order for the hook to penetrate the fish's mouth and achieve a secure hook-up. Remember, the bigger the fish the tougher the mouthparts, and the more difficult it is to sink the hook past the barb.

Fighting:

Your reel's drag needs to be set appropriately before you begin fishing. A rule of thumb is to set the drag at one-third the pound test of the line. So, if you are using ten-pound test line, a drag of about three pounds is good. If you are using twenty-pound test line, the math gives us a drag of six to seven pounds. It isn't important to strictly adhere to the one-third rule when we use stronger lines. Consider that a seven-pound drag can pull a small car, so a four-pound drag is more than enough to fight a large bluefish or striper in open water. However, increase the drag when fishing around obstructions such as docks, buoys, and rock piles.

Please don't fish with a one-pound drag or, even worse, less than one-pound of drag. Are you laughing? Well, don't laugh because I encounter this all the time. Remember the anecdote above about the guy who let a twenty-pound striper swim around helter-skelter? What do you think his drag was set at? It wasn't four pounds I can assure you. A drag setting of about one-pound allows a fish the latitude to just run around. In addition, the angler will experience very little of a fish's fighting ability, and it also becomes more and more difficult to release a fish fought and landed this way. The fellow's rod, by the way, only had a modest bend during the fight, in spite of the fact that the fish weighed about twenty pounds. That's another sign that his drag was far too loose.

On the other hand, proper tackle fished with a proper drag not only is sporting, but also allows an angler to participate, experience, and enjoy the fight. Most experienced skilled anglers want to test the mettle of a fish and experience the excitement of the power of the fish. Just hanging on to a fish is boring to most seasoned anglers, and the same anglers also believe the approach disrespects the fish. North American Indians really found something important when they developed an ethic of respecting the targets of their hunts. Every action was refined to honor and respect the animals they hunted, ate, and ultimately revered. We would all do well to adopt a similar philosophy.

In any event, I follow a philosophy of fighting them tough because I don't simply want to be attached to a fish; I want to make a fish fight as hard as it can because it's the hits and the fights that I signed up for. Fight them tough and have more fun.

Landing:

Landing fish also seems to intimidate some anglers or, perhaps they are lost about what to do. There are two ways to land a fish, and both approaches are easily done. The essence of landing a fish includes working with the physical environment and bearing in mind the safety of both angler and fish.

With Your Hands:

When I'm standing in the water, such as when I fish in the quiet waters of back-bays, sounds, and inlets, I stand in the water up to my thighs and land the fish where I stand. Now, there is a caveat associated with the approach and that is I will not handle or land big fish, especially big bluefish, while standing in the water. However, bass up to ten pounds and blues up to about six pounds can be managed safely in the water if you have an appropriate tackle setup, if you have a leader to work with, and you are a practiced angler.

I always wear gloves. In warmer weather I wear woven cotton gloves with small gripping dots on the palm side of the glove. These gloves are widely sold in convenience stores and are inexpensive. When a fish tires a bit and comes close to me, I lift the rod tip so that the fish is encouraged to slide towards me on the surface. Typically, I make this move when there's a rod's length of line between the tip-top and the fish. Now I make one backhand wrap around the leader so that I can easily allow the leader to unwind off my hand, if the fish unexpectedly makes a sudden charge. Once my wrap is secure and the mouth of the fish is above the waterline, I'm ready to remove the hook. I tuck my rod under my arm if I'm using a lure with a single hook, grab the fish to secure it; either behind the head on the dorsal side if it's a blue, or lip a striper, so I can easily remove the hook. If I'm using a lure with treble hooks, I'll slide my nine-inch needle-nose pliers from my belt pouch and use the pliers to disengage the treble hooks while holding the leader with my other hand, one hook at a time. Be patient. Smaller fish won't usually need reviving if the reel's drag was set appropriately, and thus the fish can be released quickly without a major risk of injury or mortality.

Using the Beach:

The ocean surf is rougher more often than are backwaters, and decent size waves often eliminate the chance to stand waist deep in the water. In the ocean surf, we usually stand back a ways so that crashing and receding waves don't knock us down and drag us out to sea. However, the sloped sand and the waves that roll in can become assets to help us land fish if an angler exercises a little patience.

As a fish approaches the surf zone (the sloped sand where waves crash), prepare to use the waves that roll up the slope, and recede. Try to develop a sense of the frequency and pattern of the waves. When a fish turns broadside to a receding wave, don't try to reel line in. Instead allow the pressure of the water on the fish to pull out line against the drag. If the pressure becomes too great because the fish is large, walk toward the fish at the moment when the pressure is greatest. When the wave has receded and the incoming wave begins to lift, use the surge of the incoming wave to help move the fish towards you. When the wave pushes in, tension on the line will be least and at this point lift your rod to pull the fish towards you, and then lower the rod tip while at the same time reeling in line. Perform this up and down motion in such a way that a slight bend remains in the rod in order to sustain a tight connection to the fish as you slowly lower the rod tip. Repeat this again and again.

So, to summarize, allow the receding waves to pull line off the reel, but keep your rod tip pointing towards eleven o'clock not at the fish, and when the next wave rushes up the beach, use an up and down motion of your rod as described above, and reel in line on the downbeat.

Eventually the time will come when the fish is quite far up the slope of the beach and pressure from receding waves becomes less and less powerful. I see many anglers make two kinds of mistakes at this point. The first mistake is to attempt to pull the fish across the sand. This works okay when the fish is small, but bigger fish sink into the sand a bit and will not slide over the sand, but instead begin to plow the sand. The second mistake I often see involves rushing into the surf zone to try and grab at the leader or the fish. The turbulence is too unpredictable and strong in the surf zone to make this a safe and convenient method of landing a fish, unless it's a calm day, of course. The turbulence will push the fish one-way and then in another direction faster than most of us can react. Waves and surge will push fish against our legs and that often means a spine or a hook point penetrates our waders. Be patient and wait for the thin remnant of the next wave to slosh around your fish and lift it a little so that you can hydroplane the fish higher onto the slope. At this point, pull on the rod and the fish will glide to a much higher point on the beach where it can be more conveniently secured.

Unhooking A Fish:

A sportsman understands that when a fish is out of the water it is suffocating. Therefore, a sport fisherman moves quickly and decisively to remove the hook or hooks from the fish. I always go by a personal rule that matches the time of my breath holding with that of the fish. So, I hold my breath from the moment I lift the fish out of the water and when I can't hold my breath anymore, I know the fish can't either. Before that happens, I do all I can to remove the hook as fast as possible. Often, that's a quick process, especially if my lure has a single hook. For example, remove a bucktail by grabbing the lead-head and pushing against the bucktail so that the force is exerted down the shaft of the hook and in a direction opposite to the point of the hook. Often, I make this move with a sudden application of force that pops the hook out.

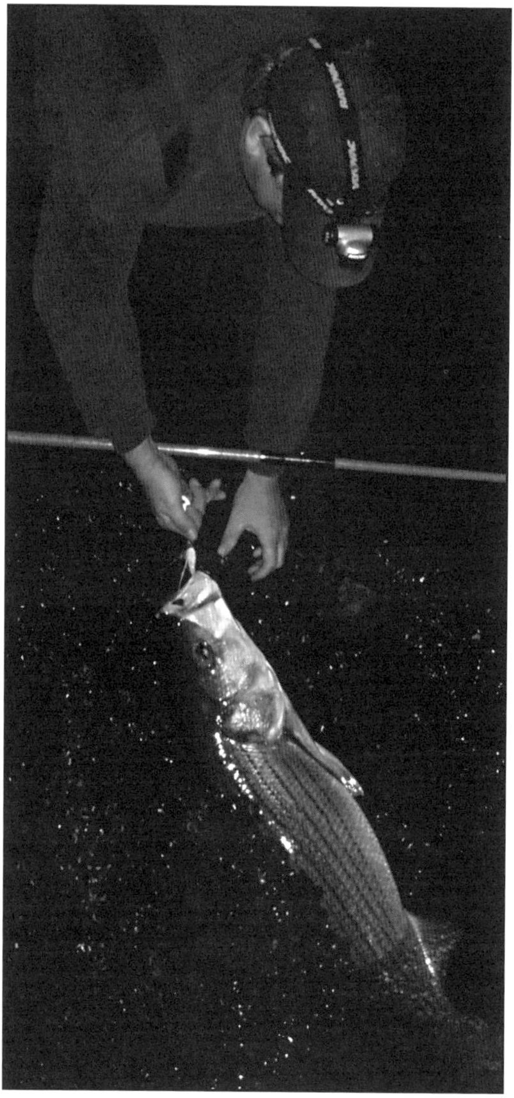

Needle nose pliers assist in the removal of well set hooks. (Zeno Hromin photo)

Single hooks in awkward places or treble hooks can be removed easily by using a nine-inch needle nose pliers. Grab the bend of the hook with the tips of the pliers and pull in a direction opposite to the hook point. If necessary, if a fish is hooked in a complex way, twist the hook or straighten the hook to get it removed quickly because the more time a fish spends out of the water, the more likely it will die within three days. If necessary because hook removal is taking too much time, put the fish back into shallow water and allow it to breathe while you catch your breath and then resume hook removal. Don't be timid about the hook removal process since a fish can heal its wounds, but cannot overcome suffocation.

Summary:

1. Fighting and landing fish are skills that many anglers view as not being skills at all. Yet, as with all other facets of angling, they are abilities that can enhance an angler's success if developed, or lead to heartache if neglected.
2. It is difficult to hook, fight, and land fish with confidence, control, and enjoyment without quality tackle to assist you.
3. I suggest you adopt a philosophy of fighting the fish tough in order to maximize the fight and fun of the battle.
4. Two ways to land a fish:
   a. Standing waist deep and using your rod, leader, and pliers.
   b. Stand back in rough water and use the waves and beach slope to help land the fish.
5. Remove hooks quickly. Small wounds will heal quickly. So, it's better to rip a hook out than let a fish suffocate.
6. Remember that a little blood looks a lot worse than it is, especially when mixed with water. Fish have a better ability to heal wounds than most humans do.

Chapter 16
CATCH & RELEASE: THE RIGHT WAY

Why Should I? Recent History and the Inevitable Reality.

Few anglers thought about catch and release in saltwater fifty years ago. Of course, there were many fewer anglers, a lot more fish of many species, and commercial fishing was a mere shadow of its present form. Gradually times changed, and so too technology. During the 1960s, for instance, foreign factory ships appeared off our shores with new electronics, better gear, and the ability to stay on the fish for weeks or months at a time. Although these ships fished on the continental shelf, their harvests began to affect the quality of recreational fishing for a number of species including mackerel, cod, haddock, yellowtail flounder, pollock, fluke, seabass, porgy, whiting, ling, and squid.

In the 1970s anglers, appreciating the impact of drastically increased foreign pressure on our fish stocks, pushed for a 200-mile exclusion limit. Eventually, these efforts were successful and the Magnuson Act was passed in 1976 and implemented in 1977. The law set up criteria for foreign harvest on our continental shelf (out to 200 miles), established regional fisheries management councils, and created incentives for domestic commercial fishermen to expand the U.S. fleet.

There's such a thing as the Law of Unintended Consequences that states that bad things often result from good intentions. Therefore, one should be careful about creating new laws intended to correct a bad situation since the unknown and unintended consequences of such laws can turn out to be devastating. That was certainly true for the 200-mile limit law. Concerned sportsmen had no desire to see the domestic commercial fleet expanded, nor did they want foreign vessels to be able to fish under a permit system. Rather, sportsmen and conservationists wanted to stop excessive harvests and protect our fisheries. However, because the law was put under the supervision of the U.S. Department of Commerce, provisions in the Magnuson Act were devoted to an expansion of the U.S. domestic commercial fishing fleet as well as to maximizing potential economic benefits for U.S. citizens involved in the fishing industry. These were clearly unintended consequences. The law should have been administered and supervised by a new cabinet department, in my opinion, free from the demands of those who desired to make money off saltwater living resources. People who make a living from fish and other living resources should be allowed to provide opinions and suggestions, but the implementation and supervision of management regimens should be directed and effected by scientists and managers who are separate from, and free of the influence of politicians and the commercial sector. Only then can management be based on what's best for the fish, the ecosystems, and the environment. In such a system, living resources flourish and ultimately so too the people who interact with those resources.

The Down Side Of Magnuson:

It is no accident that under the Magnuson Act, stocks of fish continued to decline precipitously. This led to an accelerated chain reaction because so many of the affected species spend a portion of the year in inshore waters where they are pursued by recreational anglers. As the numbers of these fish declined, pressure on the remaining species, still in relatively good shape, increased sharply. Consider the case of striped bass which benefited from sensible management restrictions in the 1980's and began to recover. Stripers became the victims of more and more pressure because so many other traditional recreational species were no longer plentiful and worth the effort to target. Thus, as I write this book, striped bass stocks have begun to decline seriously again, documented abuses have mounted, managers have failed to stay ahead of the downward curve, and many bureaucrats refuse to admit that stocks have declined or that recruitment (spawning contributions) has been generally poor or horrible. As of this writing, the same bureaucrats have taken no action and there is no sign that any conservation efforts will be forthcoming in the near future. If one projects the consequences of current poor recruitment and declining stocks on the future, we can appreciate that these facts bode poorly for both recreational fishermen and the businesses they support.

Clearly, we are again at a crucial phase in coastal fisheries management. This is not just my opinion, but articles in numerous magazines, including various editions of The Fisherman magazine, have published cautionary editorials on the subject. So, what can anglers do about this? First, become active in local organizations that fight for fisheries conservation and the sport of fishing. Two, talk to your local bait and tackle shop owners and point out that the stocks of stripers are decreasing, the bluefish population is getting smaller, the flounders are practically gone, and the future for weakfish is very obscure. Remind them that if there are less fish to catch anglers will not be motivated to spend their money on tackle, bait, or party and charter boats. After all, in the end, we fish for fun, excitement, and a sense of belonging to an association of humans that is bigger than ourselves and in whom we share a brotherhood of spirit, sportsmanship, and a belief in the need for all of us to be good stewards of the sea.

Finally, anglers can demonstrate a commitment to the long-term health of many species by practicing catch and release. To clarify, that doesn't mean an angler can't keep a fish or two to enjoy with their family from time-to-time, but time-to-time doesn't mean we keep every fish the law allows. It means we practice a selective harvest for our immediate family, but not for friends, neighbors, relatives, and some guy on the beach walking behind us who asks for a fish. It means we report those who break the law. It means we demand that our police provide better and more widespread enforcement. It means we demand that all judges impose maximum fines and or sentences on those who break these fisheries laws. By the way, if you don't know, it is not unusual for judges to dismiss fisheries violations proclaiming that when fisheries violations are matched against murder, rape, and drug dealing the importance of such environmental laws seems to take a back seat. As a result, summons for fisheries violations are often treated as trivial tickets.

That's why we need a new judicial system. We need a fish and wildlife court system with one court per county that hears nothing else but cases involving fish and wildlife violations. The judges that hear these cases need orientation sessions so that they can understand the importance of our living marine resources on the local ecosystems, environment, the quality of our recreation, and the many local family businesses that provide goods and services to recreational anglers. It is only in this way that the proper message can be sent to the public and to our elected officials. With a clear and unified voice we can begin to protect these resources properly, and initiate the process of removing management responsibility from bureaucrats who are too concerned with their own careers, and replace them with true managers free to protect and conserve our living resources. Furthermore, these courts, if run correctly, could generate enough funds not only to be self-sufficient, but also perhaps to support increased enforcement of our marine resource laws.

Grass Roots Uprising:

I believe we need a grass roots movement to force changes that will save our fisheries as well as the saltwater recreational fishing industry. Perhaps a movement to better represent the needs of both fish and people, like the Tea Party movement in politics. Certainly there are more citizens armed with a greater diversity of political information today than in recent decades, thanks to the Tea Party movement. That movement resulted in an Election Day that sent a clear message to our elected officials. A similar movement in the saltwater angling arena might awaken bureaucrats and politicians that we're fed up with roller coaster fisheries, as well as fisheries that seem to disappear like winter flounder and weakfish. Certainly, we can do a better job. It is, ultimately up to us! Although a list of positive actions that anglers can take to improve our fisheries is listed above, we should in my opinion begin our commitment with a catch and release ethic.

Support the head with one hand and hold the fish firmly with the other when reviving large fish.

How To Properly Release Fish:

A catch and release ethic begins with an appreciation of a few basics. The first is an appreciation of the importance of using quality tackle. The second is an understanding that catch and release myths are just that, MYTHS! The third is angler anticipation of the moment of decision, and the fourth, is a commitment to apply sound angling techniques. Fifth is an angler's willingness to become educated about the needs of fish and the limitations on their survival.

Let's regress for a moment to the third issue of awareness: the moment of decision. I believe that my long-time friend Roger Martin offered the best commentary on this subject many years ago. Roger is a very good surf angler, an intelligent man, a conservationist, and a thoughtful, considerate human being. I've heard him speak to young people and new anglers and urge them to think about the decision to keep or release a fish well in advance of the actual moment of the catch. He suggests that the decision becomes more difficult as the fish get bigger. He points out that the emotions and excitement of the moment are difficult to sort out quickly in the time-compressed moment of decision. On the other hand, Roger explains, sorting out what we want to do in advance; in the cool-headed time before the actual catch, makes for a quick, easy, and unconfused decision at the exact moment when a clear decision is needed. You make your decision way in advance and not when the fish lies on the sand at your feet.

In order to make the right decision and execute it effectively, it is important for anglers to have a comprehensive understanding of all the factors affecting catch and release: the fish, ourselves, and the ecology of the inshore ocean. For example, even if an angler uses proper tackle and understands the catch and release technique, setting the reel's drag too light voids anything else the angler might do to release the fish successfully. I've seen scientific reports and journal articles that indicate a catch and release mortality may be as high as 80% among anglers who do it poorly, and far less than 10% among anglers who do it right. Thus, as sportsmen, it behooves us to learn to do it right. Here are some key points to help us "do it right."

Before reviewing the things you can do to successfully release fish, understand that big fish need more attention than little ones that can simply be returned to the water with little or no reviving. The following factors apply to fish of all sizes, but are especially important when releasing large fish.

Do It Fast:

Fight fish hard and remove hooks quickly. The longer a fish is out of water, the greater the stress on the fish and the greater the chance it will die within three days. If a hook is deeply embedded into mouth cartilage or bone, rip it out rather than spend precious minutes attempting to remove the hook cleanly. Contrary to myth, most fish in temperate waters have an incredible capability to heal and recover. Just last year I caught a twelve-

An erect dorsal fin is an indicator of a fish that's ready to be released. (Zeno Hromin photo)

pound bluefish that looked as if it had been bitten by a shark. A foot-long, five-inch deep opening was on its flank. The huge wound had already begun to heal over at the edges. Although I could see the fish's stomach and intestines, it was strong, eating, and seemed to be able to keep up with its peers. So, don't worry about a small rip or tear around the mouth or a little blood, because in the scheme of things it's trivial.

Use Your Hands:

DO NOT STEP ON, OR KNEEL ON the fish when securing them or unhooking them. Instead use your hands, the leader, and pliers to perform the task properly and safely. If you're afraid of the spines of a striper or the teeth of a bluefish, you shouldn't be fishing for them. It isn't difficult or dangerous to handle these fish as described in this book.

DO NOT DROP KICK FISH into the water. Take the time to grasp them and place them into the water gently.

If a fish swallows a hook, don't try to get the hook out. The hook is cheap, the fish's strong acidic digestive juices will dissolve the hook quickly, while getting the hook out will create significant tissue damage and bleeding. Hemorrhaging is the worst part of the damage for a fish.

Big Waves:

Releasing fish in big water is more difficult than in calm waters, but the difficulties shouldn't stop us from a good catch and release. Let the surging water in breaking and receding waves do most of the work of reviving the fish. I like to walk about halfway down the slope of the beach or as far as is safe to walk. I always wear both a foul weather top and waist belt in rough water so I can maneuver down the slope until I'm about knee deep. Again, small fish can be released by gently dropping them into the water. Large fish, of course, must be revived. I hold the fish in the water by the lower jaw with a firm grip. I use two hands if necessary. I point the fish into the flow of water and thus water enters the mouth and exits through the gills. I use the same indicators of recovery described below, so when the fish's dorsal fin is erect and the fish struggles to get away, I let the fish go. It only takes a few minutes, but it's worth the effort.

Releasing fish in big water is more difficult than in calm water, but that shouldn't deter us from a proper release. (Zeno Hromin photo)

In the Water:

Although small fish don't fight hard enough when appropriate tackle is appropriately used, as previously stated, large fish require different consideration. Small fish can simply be gently dropped into the water.

Take your time with large fish. Place the fish in the water with one hand under the chin and slightly back towards the gills, and the other hand around the tail. Move the fish gently forward and backward so that water moves into the mouth and over the gills. Support the fish so that the fish's back (dorsal surface) points up and the stomach toward the sand. If possible walk a fish forward or hold the fish with its mouth into the current.

Look for Signs of Recovery:

1. Erect dorsal fins. Since the muscles that support the dorsal spines are weak, they tend to collapse first when the fish is tired, and become erect last when proper oxygen levels return to the blood.
2. Undulations of the tail as tail muscles recover from fatigue.
3. Strong surges. Strong enough that if you weren't holding the fish firmly, it would pull out of your grasp.
4. The ability of the fish to remain upright when you loosen your grasp.
5. Don't be impatient. Wait for the signs of recovery.

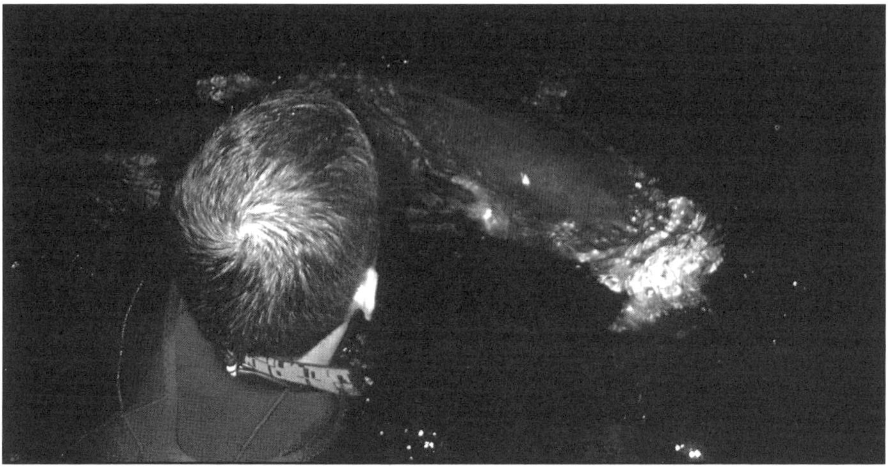

It isn't often necessary to go to extremes to release fish, but I praise the angler who does. (Zeno Hromin photo)

When these signs are manifested, you may release the fish. If the fish goes belly up, lies on its side, or on the bottom, resume your grasp and continue reviving. As long as the gill covers open and close rhythmically, the fish can most likely be revived.

Family Legacy:

Finally, let's remember that today's release is tomorrow's catch. Let's remember that today's releases are the trophies of our children and grandchildren. Let's remember that we fish for FUN and that selective restrained harvest is in the best interest of all sportsmen anglers. As adults, let's remember that it is our responsibility to teach our children about sportsmanship and a conservation ethic.

Summary:

1. Recent declines in fish stocks and generally poor management approaches mandate sportsmen to be proactive in catch and release.
2. We need a judicial system willing to support fisheries conservation.
3. Unhook and release quickly.
4. Do not step on, or kneel on fish.
5. Do not kick fish back into the water.
6. Proper tackle, used properly facilitates catch and release.
7. Support the fish in the water and be patient. Wait for recovery signs.
8. Consult the signs of recovery (above) to guide the angler about when to let go of the fish.

Chapter 17
FOUR-WHEEL DRIVE ON THE BEACH

An Accessory To Surf Fishing:

Four-wheel drive vehicles provide another dimension to surf fishing that many surf rats enjoy. It isn't a necessary element of the sport the way a rod and reel combination is, but it can add to the fun, the excitement, and also open new access areas for you. I've owned a four-wheel drive vehicle for decades, but I have never discounted the value of my feet in my angling success. Some years, I use my truck on the beach a lot, and other years very little, depending upon the feeding habits of the fish and the patterns of baitfish and gamefish movements along the beach. I've never allowed myself to become lazy because of the convenience of a four-wheel drive vehicle. I can tell you that I've caught many times more fish while walking compared to fishing from my four-wheel drive unit. I've always believed that we see more, hear more, notice more, and work more structure when we walk than when we drive.

As with so many aspects of angling, anglers with four-wheel drive vehicles have a responsibility to secure the correct permits, conform to the rules and regulations as described on the permits, respect the ecology of the beach, and show proper beach etiquette while driving on the sand and while fishing.

Where:

Four-wheel drive vehicles are allowed in a number of venues on the east coast. These include some townships, some county parks, many state parks, and the National Seashore. Check under the government pages in the phone book for the appropriate contact agency for inquiries about whether four-wheel drive vehicles are permitted on the beach and about the required permits. Read your permits carefully prior to going on the beach the first time. In some cases, anglers are required to watch a

Four wheel drive vehicles are excellent accessories to the sport of surf fishing. (Russ Paoline photo)

brief video that reviews safety, equipment, beach courtesy, regulations, and explanations about how to avoid getting stuck and how to get out should you become stuck.

Never drive in water or on sand with a "shimmer" because the shimmer effect probably means the sand contains lots of water, is soft, and represents a sink trap for your vehicle. You know what I mean. We've all walked along a beach and suddenly sunk into one of these soft sand pits. I know that I've sunk up to my knees or beyond a number of times. This is especially true after a storm.

Air Down, Air Up:

It is important to air down before going on the beach to protect your vehicle and to achieve maximum traction. The sand's characteristics change throughout the season. For example, in summer when heat extracts moisture from the sand quickly and there is little rain, the sand turns "sugary." That is, the beach is soft, the tiny grains of sand have little affinity for each other and don't cling to each other, and the turning of tires tends to push sand away from under the tire quickly. For

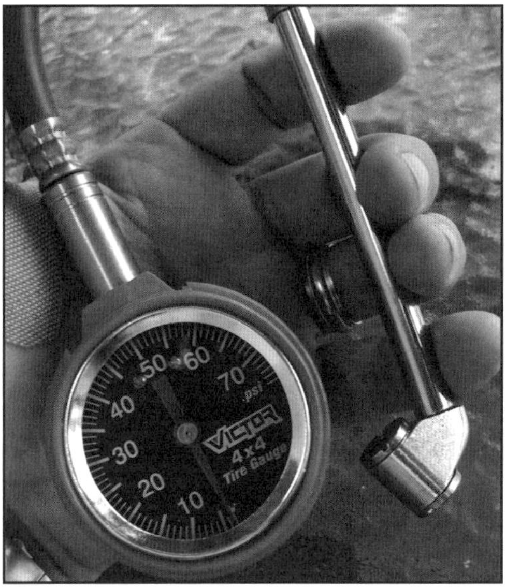

The use of an accurate gauge makes airing down and airing up more convenient. (Russ Paoline photo)

that reason, experienced anglers run the beach at a lower pressure in summer than in the fall when cooler temperatures and more frequent and heavy rains pack sand down. In autumn, the sand grains have more affinity for each other with less air between the grains. The result of these conditions is greater traction. Local regulations and or recommendations should be consulted before venturing onto the sand.

The idea is to float on sand rather than grip it. Tires with aggressive treads grab the sand and then throw it out from under the tire, causing the vehicle to sink into that space. Do not equate getting traction in snow with getting it on sand because these are two different animals. We try to create a grip on snow, but we need to float on sand. Thus, the width of a tire rather than the depth of its tread aids in traversing the sand. The weight of a truck has an effect too, as does the torque of its transmission and drive chain. Go easy in the sand. Years ago I had a manual transmission vehicle. The engine and transmission produced a lot of torque in low gears, so I started in second gear to reduce the torque and avoided "digging in."

So, know your vehicle and the manufacturers recommendations, local regulations, the condition of the beach sand, and suggestions from those who are experienced at running on that beach before deciding how much to air down. In any event, do not run at normal tire pressure. Today many, if not most, beaches are equipped with air-up stations. An angler typically needs to carry an air hose with a terminal connector for the tire valve on one end, and a male adaptor to the female port at the station. Hoses with appropriate adaptors to the tires and the air station are available in many locations including hardware stores and large home service centers. Although three-quarter inch is common, check on the size of the adaptors being used by your local air stations. Also carry a tire pressure gauge so that you can conveniently and accurately air down and up to the appropriate tire pressure.

If the beaches in your area do not provide air up stations, portable compressors are sold in many stores and are quite compact. Typically, these portable units fill tires slowly compared to permanent air station compressors, but they are worth having and using where air stations are not provided. Years ago, vehicles had a lot more room under the hood. Many of us adapted an old refrigerator compressor to the job of airing up. We bolted it to the side of the engine compartment, used an additional belt off the engine shaft (similar to the belt for the radiator fan), and some of us even added an on-off switch. However, modern computerized engines with anti pollution devices fill that space.

Servicing:

Just a reminder to consult your vehicle's service manual for the type and frequency of service recommended for the transmission, front wheel bearings, and any other special servicing suggestions when vehicles are used on the beach. Fortunately for the owners of recent vintage vehicles, the new technology and mechanics used in these vehicles requires less servicing. The extra attention to service is necessary because driving on the beach is more demanding on the vehicle's engine and transmission.

Driving On The Beach:

The permits I know about all impose low speed limits: typically ten or fifteen miles per hour maximum speed. There are many good reasons for these speed limits. One, low speeds offer a safety margin against unexpected track variations, debris, and sudden side to side truck movements that can occur when tires engage the sides of the track. Second, airing down and low speeds help to protect the integrity of the beach, reduces erosion potential, and helps to protect sea birds that nest and feed on the sand. Third, low speeds protect your transmission and drive train. Radiator and transmission temperatures run higher when on the sand because mechanical parts work harder against a moving surface than against a firm one. The faster the speed, the faster the parts turn, and generally the hotter the engine and transmission run.

Courtesy is another matter on the beach. Stay in the track as much as possible, leave plenty of room between passing vehicles, go slow, give the right of way where indicated by permit regulation or convention, and help fellow anglers in difficulty. Do not stop in the sand track; rather pull out of the way when you stop to fish. Do not attempt to make sharp turns in the sand because this will cause the sidewalls to plow sand and usually causes the rear tires to dig deeper into the sand. Take your time and make slow wide turns.

Local Four-Wheel Drive Organizations:

I recommend you join a local group devoted to protecting beach access, promoting safety, and educating its members. Many organizations also work with local permit granting agencies. On Long Island, where I live, that organization is The *Long Island Beach Buggy Association* or LIBBA. I'm a member

Observing regulations protects the beach and makes driving on the beach safer. (Zeno Hromin photo)

and I support their tireless efforts on behalf of all four-wheel drive anglers. Our support ensures that these organizations will continue to work for our angling and four-wheel driving rights.

Summary:

1. Four-wheel drive vehicles can enhance the surf fishing experience.
2. Always air down before going on the beach. Air stations are common at many access points. Get your own hose.
3. Follow the service recommendations for the four-wheel drive mechanics on your vehicle. Driving on the sand is stressful on vehicles.
4. Go slow to reduce strain on your vehicle and promote safety.
5. Know about proper beach etiquette.
6. Permits are available from federal, state, county, and town agencies.

Chapter 18
AN EFFICIENT STRATEGY

The Objective:

Repeating the same techniques and activities over and over without adequate positive results should suggest to the angler that change is in order. Whether the repetition involves the same spot, the same cast, the same timing, or the same lures doesn't matter, changes need to be made.

One of the habits I notice among beach anglers is the twilight approach to selecting a time to head down to the beach. An angler who keeps a good log and studies the notations in that log might notice that productivity during twilight trips seems to swing up and down much like a seesaw. A graphing of the angler's results might show that for a day or two during a particular week success might be good, while the next week few fish are caught. Then typically, the same up and down pattern of success repeats in the next two weeks. A closer look at the data might reveal a connection between a particular tidal period and success or failure. Twilight, both dawn and dusk, is a productive time of day, but a bad tide is a bad tide regardless of the time of day. Inversely, a good tide is a good tide regardless of the time of day. Therefore, although twilight is a great time for fishing, it isn't nearly as good when good tides don't match the time of day. I fish stages of tides that my log indicates are productive and I avoid those tidal stages when my log says few fish are caught. Thus, I might fish twilight one week and the middle of the day the next week.

Areas Differ:

Different areas produce fish at different times in a tide depending upon how water flows, the contours of the shoreline, the movements of bait, the depth of the water, and the effects of moon phases. Therefore, it's important for anglers to become

Although sunset and sunrise are productive times of the day, they work best when they coincide with the best portion of the tide. (Zeno Hromin photo)

familiar with local patterns and to understand the windows of opportunity that open and close during a tide in a particular place.

This discussion has been offered to support my philosophy of fishing tidal windows of opportunity rather than fishing the same time of day. As I said, I fish tides, not times of the day or night. However, in order to be productive in daylight, twilight, or at night, I devote a lot of time to zeroing in on windows of opportunity. Some windows last a few hours, others an hour or so, and still others only a fraction of an hour. Once I identify these windows, I schedule my trips to match the windows. Again, a "good tide" is a "good tide" regardless of when it occurs, although a good tide at dawn or dusk has the advantage of low light levels and that tends to enhance the productivity of the good tide. A "bad tide" on the other hand, is a "bad tide" no matter when it occurs. That applies to night tides, too. So, if the good tide coincides with a clock period of 2 am to 4 am, then that's when an angler should fish.

Changing The Odds:

It is helpful to understand that the odds against success in surf fishing are greater than when angling from a boat because often the water is shallower and the fish tend to avoid shallow water. Surf rats also suffer from a lack of mobility. Yes, we can drive laterally and we can walk laterally, but if the fish are just on the outside of the offshore bar, they might as well be in China. Therefore, smart beach anglers do everything possible to reduce the odds against them and improve the odds of success.

The ability to predict an angler's success in the surf is in the details. If we address these details and understand them better, we can add them to a list of particulars that improves our chances of success. The road to success may begin with our tackle selections or wander through mazes of fishing reports, but it ends in the details about lines, knots, sharp hooks, and the execution of our strategies. I pay attention to every detail I can identify because I believe in Murphy's Law. You know Murphy, the guy who said that if something can go wrong, it will. The more wrong stuff I can anticipate, the fewer potential opportunities for good old Murphy to be right.

I'm not nagging when I repeat the importance of addressing tackle, line, knots, hooks, swivels, snaps, presentations, etc, because until the significance of these details embeds itself in the brain of an angler, success will inevitably be restricted. I've met many anglers who believe they are successful, but have never considered how much more successful they would be if they worked on details.

Summary:

1. Fish tides.
2. Pay attention to details.
3. Develop a sound strategy.
4. Make the most of your opportunities.
5. Learn about windows of opportunities in your local waters.

Chapter 19
NIGHT VS. DAY

Reasons:

Why do some surf fishermen elect to fish during the day while others prefer the night? Actually, there are lots of reasons for their preferences. There are the issues of seasons, family obligations, jobs, convenience, vacations, adaptations to the night or day conditions, sleep requirements, as well as their depth of love of the sport.

I know that for more than twenty years I fished either exclusively at night or mostly at night because of my job's responsibilities and the demands of a young family. I was fortunate when I was young because I adapted well to little sleep, while others staggered in fatigue under heavy workloads, and without adequate sleep they were unable to recover before the next fishing trip. Other people are retired or self-employed and can manipulate responsibilities and schedules so that they are able to select day or night tides to fish. The decision to fish at night or during the day is a choice, but it is a choice complicated by responsibilities and schedules. In the end, we all try to carve windows of time for our hobbies from a twenty-four hour day.

Seasonal Considerations:

Without doubt the best daytime opportunities occur in the early and late parts of the season. In spring, especially late spring, a sudden influx of fish and bait triggers feeding binges that often continue through both day and night tides. A similar thing occurs in the autumn, when migrating shoals of bait must swim in open water. Combine these vast areas of dense bait with ravaging appetites induced by hormonal changes signaling the fall migration, and intense feeding competition results. In this smorgasbord of food and competition, fish feed heavily

Late spring through early fall offer less opportunity for day time success. (David Ryng photo)

both day and night.

The late spring, summer, and early fall on the other hand offer many fewer opportunities for daytime angling success. At these times, bait is small, it is huddled deep in protected shallows, water temperature is higher inducing lethargy, predator metabolisms are less demanding, their activity levels are reduced, and there is no migration pressures yet. Under these conditions, gamefish feed less often, for shorter periods, and are much more selective about what they choose to eat. Bigger fish, especially, seem to prefer to feed at night when boat traffic and other sources of human noise and commotion are diminished, the shallow water cools a few degrees, and baitfish are more vulnerable. There are dedicated groups of surf rats committed to plying bays, sounds, inlets, and sometimes the oceanfront at night seeking quality fish, but not expecting blitzes.

Problems:

In addition to sacrificing sleep, this night owl cadre of surf anglers must contend with other problems. The bug problem is a big issue; more so today because of concerns about Equine Encephalitis, Bird Flu, and West Nile Fever. Years ago, when I engaged in the bulk of my night sorties, we only worried about the itchy and swollen remnants of bug bites, and never about disease. There are remedies, of course, but some come with potential hazards. Bug repellents, for example, come in two forms: those without DEET that are safe, and those with DEET that are not. Regular long-term use of DEET repellents may have serious effects. Avon's Skin So Soft was, and to some extent continues to be, touted as an efficient repellent, and it is. However, similar to other forms of repellents, they only work efficiently if you don't perspire. That's a neat trick in warm weather or when hyped-up with adrenaline while fighting fish.

Smoke is an effective repellent even if you perspire, however, the dangers of smoking have been well documented, and I would not advocate smoking as a means of bug control.

Head netting is available, but many anglers have issues with the netting that are serious enough to turn them against using the device. There is no doubt that the netting reduces air circulation and therefore it can get hot under the mesh. The mesh affects vision acuity too, and the impairment is worse at night when there's little light. Vision impairment is not just inconvenient, it is also a safety issue affecting casting, unhooking fish, and when walking in the dark.

At certain times of the year abundant migrating bait turns daytime tides into productive intervals.

One's perspective and depth perception change at night. Some things appear to be closer than they are while others seem farther away. That sense distorts our ability to judge casting angles, where our lure is as we retrieve it, as well as the exact positions of other anglers. Distorted depth perception could cause us to take one step too many and end up falling into deeper water. Over the years, I've introduced many people to night fishing and I discovered that some people get used to it quickly, some eventually, and some people never adapt.

Staying awake can also become a serious issue. This is especially true during the drive home and can be exacerbated further by several nights of sleep deprivation. I was fortunate because coffee didn't keep me awake once I got into bed, so before beginning the drive home I'd have several cups of coffee from my thermos and perhaps a few cookies, too. Even jacked-up on caffeine, there were several times when I started to nod off, but ultimately recovered in time. It's one of the reasons I preferred to travel and fish with a friend or two. Conversation limits the likelihood of nodding off. Sometimes when I was alone I'd blast the radio or open the windows in an attempt to stay awake.

Wildlife can be another problem for night anglers. Deer, raccoons, massive stingrays, sharks, packs of feral dogs, and, unfortunately, packs of feral people out in the night for the wrong reasons. Allow me to relate several stories that perhaps are both humorous and shed light on the potential dangers.

Story 1:

It was about thirty years ago during the early fall on a beach in Long Island Sound. I caught a fish that bled out and so I kept it. It was about one in the morning and the beaches were quiet and deserted. I tossed the fish up on the beach behind me and resumed fishing. I heard rustling behind me, turned to look, saw nothing, and resumed casting. I heard the noise again. This time when I turn around I saw two bright eye retinas staring at me. The creature, whatever it was, was near my fish. I walked out of the water and shined my light on it. It was a raccoon and it had a strong hold on the head of my fish with its teeth. The critter had a few buddies. I rushed the raccoon with my arms held high, my eleven-foot surf rod thrashing about, and screaming wildly. The raccoons were not impressed and did not retreat. I paused my attack, but then resumed the forward assault. The animals continued to hiss at me, snarl, and some advanced in my direction. I stopped again. I reached out with my rod: a safe buffering distance I thought, and tried to hit the raccoons. They hissed while the one with the fish dragged it up the beach. I charged, they charged, and I decided upon a wiser course. These raccoons were serious, so I let them have the fish.

Story 2:

In another case, my buddies and I had found some trophy stripers feeding on small seabass along the shores of a south shore inlet. I was standing thigh deep in the water, attempting to reach a small sand hump with a long cast. It wasn't a full moon, but there was significant moonlight being filtered through high thin clouds. It was a great night to be fishing. Whenever my friends and I fished in an inlet, we always made a point of snatching a look behind us before each cast. We knew from experience that there were big critters swimming in the inlets, and it was easy for one of them to slide in behind us while we were preoccupied with fishing. I glanced behind me as I got set to cast, and barely noticed something, but nonetheless continued the forward swing of my rod. I never released the line off my finger and my lure thudded in front of me. I turned around slowly, shuffling my feet in tiny little pirouettes, until I saw what was behind me. Something had registered in my mind when I turned to glimpse the water behind me, but it hadn't fully alerted me. Suddenly I realized that sand isn't black, and that caused me to interrupt my cast. Indeed, a vast patch of sand behind me was black, only it wasn't sand. In the moonlight I was able to see the outlines of the beast. I held out my eleven-foot rod against the black patch of bottom. It was about as long as my rod, and almost as wide. It was a massive stingray.

Now, I wasn't worried about being bitten because that's not a stingray's thing, and I wasn't worried about being stung because I figured my thick waders would protect me from a sudden slash from the tail. However, my brain did a few calculations while evaluating the situation, and I began to realize there was a real danger.

The stingray weighed many hundreds of pounds, I was in

thigh deep water, the inlet water was rushing out at maximum speed, and, if the ray spooked, it could easily knock me off my feet and into the swirling current just a foot or so in front of me. A friend stood twenty-feet to my right as I began to make small sidesteps away from the head of the ray and towards the tail. My friend said, "What the hell are you doing?" I explained my dilemma. He began to laugh, but I found no humor in my predicament. I continued to patiently slide away from the huge ray until I was able to walk out of the water. Once on the beach, I realized that I had not taken a real breath in a while, placed my hands on my knees, and began to catch my breath. My friend continued to laugh, and the more I tried to explain, the louder he laughed until his belly laughs seemed to echo off the imaginary walls erected by the stillness of the night. Me, well I wasn't laughing because my image of possible events was different than his. I saw myself knocked off my feet by a steamroller ray, tossed into deeper water, engulfed by tidal eddies, and whirling about out to sea. From that perspective, I wasn't amused. Yes, night has its angling advantages but a few real dangers and some personal disadvantages.

Summary:

1. Fishing at night is a choice affected by many factors.
2. Fishing at night at certain times can be a shortcut to bigger fish.
3. Be prepared for tormenting bugs.
4. Realize that there are more safety issues when fishing at night compared to daytime.
5. Remember that many land animals are nocturnal and that big stripers and blues aren't the only sea creatures that are more comfortable in the shallows at night.
6. Take precautions to stay awake on the ride home.
7. Day or night, focus on perfecting your presentations.

Chapter 20
THE SPORT, EGOS, & TRADITIONS

Warriors For Marine Resources:

Sport fishing has a long tradition of sportsmanship as well as a commitment to conservation and environmental protection. The sport has also nurtured conventions about how, when, and why to do things. Over time, these conventions evolved into an ethic that includes honor and integrity. Towards that end, sportsmen have been at the forefront of speaking out when industry and commercial interests have depleted living resources and endangered our most treasured marine habitats. In some ways, surf fishing and those who practice the sport have been most vocal, perhaps because our preferred way to fish is more difficult and so easily affected by declining stocks. Whatever the reasons, surf fishermen are well represented in conservation organizations as well as on official government advisory boards at all levels. Perhaps then, we can appreciate why it is the responsibility of all surf anglers to understand our proud history and to sustain and nurture a level of dignity that respects these traditions. It has been an honor to meet and work side by side with a number of these past and present warriors for conservation and protection, and their efforts should never be forgotten. The list includes the late John Fritz and Bob Rance, and my friends and colleagues in the surf, Fred Schwab, Fred Golofaro, Willy Young, Billy Lomniki, and Chuck Hollins. There are others, and I do not intend to slight anyone, but these are the people I've worked closely with over the years and our days in the trenches are the most vivid.

Egos:

Egos are always a part of accomplishment. I never met a successful person without a strong ego. Egos drive us towards excellence, and in turn the drive improves us. No, egos aren't intrinsically evil, but some humans indulge their egos in disappointing ways. I suppose there are those who believe my ego has fluttered over the edge of preferred behavior now and again, and I apologize. However, ego-tripping has acquired a new definition in recent decades, in my opinion, and I've been distressed by it. My purpose here isn't to be critical. I don't want to chastise anglers, and I have no right to, but I do hope this discussion will stimulate some thought and a dialogue about the subject. Sometimes, individual introspection can lead to significant change that benefits many people. My principal concerns revolve around the Internet, killing fish, and the search by some for their Andy Warhol minute.

The Internet is a great tool for providing information on a huge variety of subjects. I use it, we all use it, but like so many other inventions designed to improve the human condition such as guns, automobiles, airplanes, and pharmaceuticals, they can also become tools that undermine our dignity and our respect for things and people. Here are some of the things that cross my mind on the subject. Why, I wonder, would someone who calls himself a surf angler and sportsman, then get on the Net and tell anyone who happens by the web site, where they can go to kill a mess of fish? Who are the beneficiaries? Sportsmen, conservation minded anglers, surf rats that respect the sport, other anglers, or the fish species they pursue? I think not. I'm sure that some of those who benefit are serious and appropriate, but the public nature of it invites lazy anglers, inept anglers, meat fishermen, law-breakers, and transitory participants to the right time and place. I can understand a desire to help other hard-working, dedicated, and respectful anglers and to share a good thing. However I wonder why anyone would want to provide this knowledge to people unknown to the information provider and of unknown substance and character?

The tradition I was raised in also included a desire to help fellow anglers enjoy a run of fish. But, I was warned to be judicious about sharing. I was instructed to understand a few but important criteria about sharing information. First, are the people you share information with true sportsmen, and can they be trusted with the information? If they can't be trusted they may disseminate the information to the four winds. Second, will this person use this information for self-aggrandizement, indiscriminate killing, as leverage for some other benefit, or will they be grateful for the chance to enjoy good fishing in a way that respects the sport, the fish, and the angler who put them into the fish? Third, does this angler find his or her own fish, and does that angler return the favors to others?

Jack Frech, (left) innovated new lure designs and advocated the use of wetsuits, and Fred Schwab (right) has been a warrior for striped bass conservation for decades. (High Hill Striper Club photo)

Bragging on the net makes me crazy, too. Aren't the fish enough? Aren't the joys of the sport enough? Isn't the camaraderie of other good anglers enough? What is enough? Why is there a need for endless ego-massage, and why do other respectful anglers put up with it and participate in it? I know what fish I've caught. I find no need to drag them around, weigh them in and pose for a photo with a dead fish that may never get to a dinner table. Why the need to advertise to the world that a fish was caught? I am mystified by the ego satisfying needs of some anglers who consider themselves sportsmen. Of course I share with my friends, but I do so privately where I can control who gets the information and limit it to those I know will respect my rights, the rights of the fish, and the sport. Sure, I've got an ego, and sure I enjoy it when a respected buddy says "Nice fish," but we need limits to ego gratification, don't you think?

In recent years I've experienced more and more so-called anglers who couldn't find a fish on their own with twelve nets and a box of TNT, who then brag on the Net about their prowess. It's disappointing because the fish and the sport suffer with each and every out of control ego gratification event.

The late Bob Rance led "Save Our Stripers" for many years and was a staunch advocate for striped bass conservation. (High Hill Striper Club photo)

Killing For Ego:

Too often fish are killed for the wrong reasons. I know anglers who drag every big legal fish into a tackle shop for a weigh in. What happens to the fish? Does that angler and his family members eat that fish? Perhaps sometimes, but I think many fish are given away to relatives and neighbors or worse, sold on the black market. Don't kid yourself, there's a lot of black market fish selling going on.

It is too easy to forget that every dead fish can never be caught again, that every dead fish can never spawn again, and that every fish that is killed and removed from the environment diminishes the population and thus potentially reduces the quality of our fishing experience in the future. Some years ago, I pointed out to angler who was competing in a local contest that it was illegal to kill a fish, hide it in his truck, and then keep another, and another, and another. His response was emphatic. "I keep them so you can't catch them and beat me in competition." At this point I understood the situation was hopeless, so I walked away, called the DEC (they never showed up), and hoped this guy would figure "IT" out someday.

The more fish that are returned to the water, the larger the population of that species, and the better will be the quality of our future angling experiences. That's the "IT!" Killing is a dead-end that cannot be sustained. Again, that doesn't mean an angler shouldn't keep a fish **now and then** if the fish is used properly, but the everyday mindless killing for God knows what assumed purpose is inane!

Soapbox:

I know I'm on a soap box and I know it can be tedious to read or listen to, but I believe the discussion is needed because not only do these behaviors disrespect the sport, the fish, and other sportsmen, they also exist at cross purposes to our goals. That is, we like catching fish, yet the fewer fish swimming in the water, the less likely we'll be able to catch them. That's a fact, not a myth, so why aren't we all fighting tooth and nail to keep more fish in the water? I don't understand. If someone has an explanation that makes sense, I'm listening. So, forgive me as I'm perched on my soapbox, but whether the discussion bothers you or not, it remains an important discourse.

Fortunately or unfortunately I've lived long enough to experience many ups and downs in the quality of fishing. The sad truth is that although fish populations cycle up and down, there is no need for the speed and magnitude of the declines. With better and more conservation minded management approaches, the steep declines I've witnessed in striped bass, weakfish, cod, pollock, winter flounder, and others would have been much more gentle downward sloping curves. In fact, the declines might have been so slow that by the time the bottom was reached, new year-classes might have already begun the process of reversing the curve upward. Instead, we seem to always go for the immediate "buck" or the big kill! How much better might things be for anglers, bait and tackle store owners, local tackle manufacturers, rod makers, marinas, and other businesses if fish stocks didn't drop off the charts so fast? Voting for a conservative approach to management is **always** the right thing to do.

Summary:

1. Please fish for fun.
2. Please harvest fish judiciously.
3. Don't kill fish for ego reasons.
4. Don't give fish away: let others catch their own or buy the ones that are already dead at the market.
5. Respect the sport, the fish, other sportsmen, and share information carefully and appropriately.
6. Always push managers to develop conservative management strategies.

Chapter 21
TACKLE MAINTENANCE

Wear And Tear:

The "salt" in saltwater is the main reason why marine anglers need to take more care of their tackle compared to our freshwater brethren. Add to the salt some dirt, oil and grease, and the heat and pressure generated when metal parts move against other metal parts, and a witch's brew emerges with the ability to wear down, corrode, and impede tackle function. Typically, we think first about the effects of these factors on our reels, but knots, line, rods, and lures are attacked too.

There are a host of reasons why we should be interested in maintaining and caring for our tackle. Some are grasped immediately while others either may go overlooked or only become significant to us when a disaster results from our neglect. In this chapter I'll discuss various aspects of tackle care, but I'll stay away from an obsessive attitude that for me takes away a lot of the fun of angling. That is, I know some people who spend more time cleaning and maintaining their tackle than they do fishing, and I want no part of that. I'll try to keep it simple so that the tackle benefits, but the angler isn't burdened to the point of disinterest.

Reel:

Let's begin with a recommendation that in my opinion should be everyone's individual mantra. "I shall buy and use no reel that was not designed, constructed, and intended for use in saltwater." Seriously, there are popular freshwater reels on the market and they will work in saltwater for a while, but they'll die a short corroded death and worse, they might cost you the fish of a lifetime.

Although reel manufacturers almost universally recommend that anglers rinse reels in freshwater after each trip, I'm not keen on that approach. Sure, if the reel has spent significant time underwater or been splashed on most of the tide, I'll give it a quick rinse in freshwater. However, if the contact with the briny has been limited and has dried, I'm reluctant to rinse it. I worry about salt crystals, dirt, and grime that remains behind after the water evaporates and is now "glued" to various parts of my reel. My feeling is that a freshwater rinse will act as a conduit, lift the salt and grime, dissolve the salt, and carry it deeper into the reel through small crevices. In such cases, I prefer to spray the reel thoroughly with WD 40 and then wipe it off. WD 40 displaces water and pushes it out of the reel's crevices along with dirt and salt crystals. This approach has worked for me for decades, but I wish to be clear that I am not urging angler to disobey the recommendations of the manufacturer. Rather, I'm just sharing a few ideas.

I clean my reels thoroughly and regularly in order to remove grime, water, and salt. I don't just wipe the exterior reel housing; rather I take the reel apart to the extent that its design and my expertise will allow me, and clean individual components. I also lubricate the parts with an appropriate material prior to reassembly.

Although I generally use Van Staal reels and don't feel comfortable opening them, there is still maintenance I can do.

Don't let this happen to your reel: take care of your tackle. (Zeno Hromin photo)

For example, I carefully remove and disassemble the manual roller, clean the component parts, lubricate them, and reassemble in the correct order. I also take the handle apart to clean and lubricate its parts and oil the handle bearing. I spin the cup of the reel for a while to give the light oil a chance to work into the bearing. It isn't a full-fledged lubrication, but some oil gets into the bearing. Likewise, if the drag isn't a sealed model, I disassemble the drag, clean it, and put it together. I have no illusion that I'm doing a deep thorough cleaning of my Van Staal reels. I let the factory people do that once a year. I believe my major accomplishment is to clean the accessible parts that are constantly in motion and are exposed to the elements and dirt. Clean lubricated parts don't wear against each nearly as much as when they are coated with grit and grime. Check the manufacturer's manual before disassembly and cleaning. Knowing what the components are that make up a reel part (ex. handle) and the sequence of assembly before you begin cleaning will save time, aggravation, and may also prevent the loss of tiny components. Attempt only what you are capable of.

Rod:

Many anglers neglect rod maintenance, yet salt crystals develop in the nooks and crannies of guides, reel seats, and also in micro-scratches in the finish on the rod blank. Once again, given some time, the combination of salt, oil, grit, and flexing can erode the metal, weaken a reel seat, and affect the efficiency and life span of a rod.

I rinse my rods regularly with freshwater and wipe them dry, but I don't stop there. I work Q-Tips into the corners of the guides in order to get at gunk that sticks persistently in those corners. When the rod is dry, I apply a thin layer of car wax to all the parts of the rod and then polish with a clean cloth. The wax does the same thing for my rod that it does for the finish of my truck: it protects and serves as a barrier against dirt and salt. I make certain to apply wax to the guide rings too, and wipe them with a cloth in order to maintain a smooth clean surface that reduces drag on the line as the loops of line wind their way

Using your tackle under extreme conditions requires extra care. Consult the manufacturer's product guide for details. (Zeno Hromin photo)

off the reel and through the guides. Each cleaning provides me with an opportunity to examine the rod for cracks and decay that could lead to future problems.

Line:

Braided line needs very little care. Unlike monofilament line that is scratched by use and weakened by U.V. rays and soaking in water, braided line is virtually indestructible. I have no idea how long braided line can actually last because I change it long before it's fragile. I've been extending the service of each spool-up of braid, but I haven't reached a time limit yet. Still, the braid has been on several of my reels for a few years now.

I do, however, suggest that anglers inspect the braid regularly for abrasions, knots, and frayed areas. Although it isn't necessary to cut back as often with braid as with monofilament line, remove the first few feet of braid regularly because it suffers the most abuse. Examination of tackle is the first line of defense against future problems. You can't solve a problem that you don't know exists.

Leaders:

I check my leader before and after each trip. (You can check chapter six for details about leaders). I look for brittleness, kinks, curlicues, and knot weakness. Ultimately, my leader is my connection to the lure and the fish on that lure, so I check it frequently and change my leader rather often. Leaders are easy to make and are inexpensive, so why not use fresh ones. Once again, why lose the fish of a lifetime because of an old and faulty leader with a weak spot or knot?

Hooks:

I'm fanatical about hooks. I've stated previously that poorly tied knots account for 90% of the break-offs anglers experience. Of the remaining 10%, perhaps it is true that dull hook points, rusted hooks, and weakened hooks account for 90% of that 10%.

Even the strongest and best hooks are relatively inexpensive. I buy them either in boxes of 25 or 100 and change them at the first sign of imperfection. I also sharpen my hooks before every

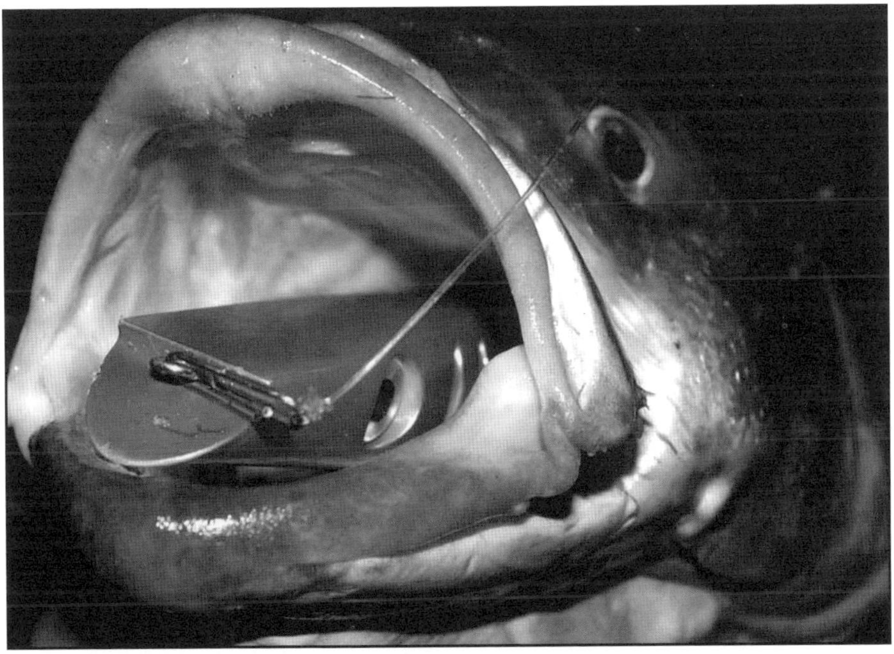

Striped bass gill covers, blue fish teeth, and rocks fray leaders and line. Check them often. (Alberto Knie photo)

trip. Yes, it's easy to sink even a dull hook into a small fish, but large fish have tough mouths with thick cartilage and bones, and sinking a hook into hard tissue can be a lot more difficult. I sharpen, I sharpen, and then I sharpen some more until the point of the hook catches my fingernail without pressure. I also carry a small sharpening device with me into the surf, and after I catch a few fish or drag a lure through the sand I check the hook for sharpness and if it is dull, I sharpen it right there on the beach. Do you get a sense that I think sharp strong hooks are very, very, important? Right!

Storing Tackle:

In season, I store my tackle so that I can get at it easily. I never leave rods and reels inside my vehicle when I'm home. I hang the rod and reel on curved rack arms, horizontally, and properly spaced, so that the rod and reel are straight and without uneven pressure. I always loosen the drag when the rod and reel are stored between trips in order to avoid any chance that drag pressure might warp the spool and permanently compress the drag washers.

Waders:

I hang my waders in the garage so they can dry and so there are no creases in the legs that could eventually become cracks and leaks. I use a spacer at the top of the waders that spreads the chest area open so that the insides can dry out.

Bucktails & Lures:

I have a low-rise plastic container set up inside my truck where I can dangle bucktails and other lures (especially bucktails) from its edge so they can dry. I remove the lures from my bag, shake them free of water, and hang them to dry. I also hang my lure bag in my garage to dry if it has become wet. This may seem imposing, but if your vehicle is set up for it, the entire process including hanging waders, bags, rods and reels, and lures takes only a few minutes.

Line:

I recommend to those using monofilament line that you store it in a dark, cool, dry place. Monofilament is affected by light, moisture, and changes in temperature. Proper storage is especially important if you have a large bulk spool. If you store mono appropriately, it will last for years.

On the other hand, I don't fuss about where I store my large spools of braid. I do take pains that these spools don't get wet, and I don't store them in my hot attic crawl space either, but barring extreme conditions, little special care is needed for braided lines.

Off Season:

I use a different approach when the fishing season is over. I take the reels off the rods, clean both rods and reels, hang the rods horizontally on the rack arms, and put the reels into boxes for the winter. If a reel needs service I send it to the manufacturer's service center immediately after the season so that in the rush of the holidays, I don't forget. Similarly, lure bags, waders, lures, and foul weather tops are inspected and cleaned. Some lures inevitably will need mending, hooks will need changing, line may need to be replaced, and new waders may be needed for the coming year. But this is winter work, and after the holidays I attack each project one at a time. It gives me "fishing stuff" to do during the winter, and besides, I'm prepared when the first stripers stir.

Summary:

1. Check the product's accompanying manual for manufacturer's suggestions on maintenance and storage.
2. I prefer WD 40 instead of water for cleaning my reels.
3. I disassemble, clean, and lubricate simple moving parts, such as the handle and drag system, regularly.
4. I clean my rods regularly, and store them horizontally on wooden hooks.

5. Braided line should be checked for frays and knots, but can be stored without special consideration. Monofilament line should be stored in a dark, cool, and dry place.
6. Check leaders frequently for nicks, frays, and signs of weakening knots.
7. Check hooks often and sharpen them before each trip.
8. Store waders by hanging them in a cool dry place.
9. Off-season cleanup should be more thorough and the equipment should be thoughtfully stored with consideration to safety, accessibility, and environmental conditions.
10. Send reels back to the manufacturer for a complete service, when needed.

Chapter 22
BAIT FISHING

What Is It?

There are two ways to fish in the surf: with artificial lures and with natural bait which can either be alive or fresh dead. Typically eels, worms, and occasionally bunker are used alive, while chunks of fresh-dead fish are probably the most often used natural bait. Anglers use special terminal rigs and sometimes employ special rod and reel combinations to cast the natural bait into the water. The cast bait settles on the bottom with the help of a sinker and does all the fishing. It is a passive form of surf fishing because once the bait is cast out, the angler waits for a passing fish to acquire the scent of the bait, home in on it, and eat it. The angler is a bystander while this is happening, but must pay attention to the spiked rod and reel, the tension on the line, and the possibility of a bite. Since it is passive and the bait does the fishing, less able anglers often gravitate toward the use of bait rather than artificial lures.

There is definitely a place for bait fishing within the sport of surf fishing, although many accomplished anglers disdain the practice. Of course, this difference of opinion often establishes a rift between those who use artificial lures exclusively and those who fish with natural bait exclusively. However, I believe there is a middle ground between the extremes.

Many anglers have contempt for anglers who use only natural bait as a means to catch a fish, rather than nurture a desire to learn and become enmeshed more deeply in this great sport. It is difficult to accept someone into the brotherhood of surf fishing when the angler seems to have little interest in surf fishing and a lot of interest in catching a fish to kill.

There is little doubt that it is easier to catch a big fish with bait than with artificial lures. That is another reason why some anglers with hot egos, hungry for a trophy fish, gravitate to bait fishing. Practiced bait fishermen have honed their bait fishing skills over many years and their approach is precise rather than haphazard the way an unskilled angler might approach bait fishing. That means the experienced angler uses a vast amount of acquired knowledge in order to use the correct tackle, understand beach structure, and use rigs that catch extremely well. He takes very good care of the bait, knows where and how to get quality bait, fishes near specific pieces of structure, and owns an understanding of how moon phases, seasons, weather conditions, and sea conditions conspire to put fish in those specific places. Sounds a lot like previous discussion about fishing with lures, doesn't it?

I apply my own ethics to bait fishing as I do to other styles of fishing. As a conservationist and catch and release sportsman, I have an obligation to fish in a manner consistent with those ethics. Therefore, on those few occasions when I fish with natural bait, I always hold my rod, react immediately to even the slightest nudge or pick-up, and set the hook immediately to help insure that I'll hook the fish in the mouth rather than deeper in the throat, or gills, or stomach. On those rare occasions when a hook ends up deep in the fish, I don't try to remove it, rather I snip the leader as close to the mouth as possible and let the fish dispose of the hook in its own way and in its own time. Consider that hooks are cheap, but fish are not.

When To Use Natural Bait:

There are a wide variety of natural baits, but in reality anglers use a short the list. As stated, the list includes chunks of various fish, worms, clams, squid, sand fleas, eels, grass shrimp, shrimp, and perhaps things I haven't thought about. I will not talk about clams because I don't like to, or sand fleas and grass shrimp because of the trouble connected with collecting and keeping them alive, nor will I discuss shrimp because they are too expensive. When I was kid and shrimp were cheap, we used them often, but at today's prices it isn't practical. Squid is okay, I guess, but there's really no advantage to using it, so why bother.

Although I prefer to fish with artificial lures, there are times when I go bait fishing. Why do I make that decision? To begin with, as with all things in angling, what you're about to read is my way, but it isn't everyone's way.

There are several key criteria that guide me in my choice. First, I begin to think about bait fishing when I have knowledge that lots of fish are accessible, but these fish will not respond to lures. That criteria can be a little tricky for some anglers with limited skills since these anglers find it easy to conclude that it isn't their skills that are at issue, rather that the fish won't take lures. Second, I'll sometimes use bait if fish are present and patrolling an area, but are quite spread out and feeding competition is low. Third, if fish are staging but not eating. At this point in my decision-making I know the fish are around and I have insight into why they won't bite on lures. I also know that, like you and me, fish are open to an easy snack or meal. They may be in a negative feeding mode, but how can you pass up a peanut? Humans can't and fish can't either.

To Illustrate:

In the 1980s for example, there were very few stripers, but there were lots of big blues, but most of the time the blues were inactive. That's right! I know many of you think blues are always easy to catch, but as previously stated, that attitude is wrong. The Cedar Bar at Fire Island Inlet in that decade had a far different structure than it did before the 80s, or after that decade. A huge sand bar stuck out into the ocean about three-quarters of a mile. It projected from the base of the Sore Thumb jetty and ran more or less parallel to the jetty at Democrat Point. Huge schools of blues were packed into a small section of ocean both on the inlet side of the bar and in the ocean off the tip of the sand. These were bruiser bluefish with typical weights ranging between fourteen and eighteen pounds, but on most days they could not be caught with lures. Only when a huge school of bait came by or when the ocean was rough, did the blues take a fancy to lures. Before long, after repeated futile attempts with every lure known to man, we discovered that they would take a chunk of bunker or mackerel. So, 90% of the time, we needed to use chunks of bait to get them to bite, and that's exactly what we did. So much for blues being easy to catch!

Rods and Reels:

Although I have conventional outfits (revolving spool reels) and I have used them for bait fishing, I tend to use eleven-foot spinning rods. I use the same one-piece medium power rods, just as I do with lures. In the 80s before graphite rods were improved and became widespread, I used an eleven-foot S-glass, but today I use the same GSB medium rod I cast lures with. The point is, whether one uses a conventional outfit or a spinning set up, use quality components. Many years ago, before graphite rods and hi-tech reels, bait fishing anglers had a definite advantage with conventional combos. I think technology has narrowed that gap considerably. Whichever tackle mode you prefer, you'll need some "teeth" designed into the equipment. Remember, most of the time you'll be casting five to eight-ounce sinkers and a fat chunk of fish or a wad of worms, so you'll need to be able put some oomph into the cast.

Quality tackle, fresh bait, and a sturdy sand spike for baiting a hook and unhooking a fish improves success. Photo by (Dennis Wulf)

Line:

I believe we have lots of choices when it comes to tackle, hooks, baits, and even the type of bait-

Bunker are favorite baits. Here bluefish pushed a bunker school into a boiling bait ball. (Robert Maina photo)

fish we use to chunk. However, I don't believe the jury is out when it comes to line. Although it is possible to successfully use braided line, I have found monofilament line to be a better choice when fishing with bait. Believe me, I tried braid and tried again, and as much as I love the stuff and use it exclusively with lures, I have to admit that monofilament is better for bait fishing. Why?

Monofilament is more forgiving. It is also less limp and it sinks. Braided line almost floats. In fact when it's dry, it does float. So, when the bait is on the bottom and waves and currents push the sinker around a little and slack gradually develops, there's a genuine tendency for the braid to rise off the bottom, kink, knot, and wander around the terminal gear. Then, there's the question of stretch. Monofilament stretches: it's inherent in the chemistry, and when fishing with lures we often see this as a negative. Yet, our hook sets when fishing with lures tend to be quick upward stabs of the rod tip. On the other hand, when we fish with bait, we drop the rod tip after sensing a pickup, and when the line goes tight we make an exaggerated upward powerful sweep of the entire rod. There are reasons why we do this. We need to sink a big hook (5/0-9/0), we need to be sure the power of the hook set drives the point through the bait chunk and into the fish, and we need to compensate for any slack that might be in the system. I believe it's easy to snap the braid doing this, not because the line can't take it, rather because of the sudden application of force focused on one point. In short, when we use braid and make a hard hook set we are snapping the line, but there's no stretch. Thus, the energy is instantly focused on the knot, or kink, or abrasion. Bang!

The next consideration about line is pound-test. Most anglers search for a compromise between line strength and casting distance. I settled on twenty-pound Trilene Big Game line because it was strong, cast well, and I had few problems with kinking and knotting.

Hooks For Chunking:

I prefer a 6/0 Siwash hook because it has a big wide bend and a long hook point that I feel allows me to achieve a secure hook up. Other anglers seem to prefer 6/0 and 8/0 Octopus style hooks. Both are good. However, I wish I could say the same for circle hooks. In an effort to fish in a manner consistent with my conservation ethic, I jumped on the circle hook bandwagon when the hooks first appeared on the market. I tried a number of manufacturers' products and I was persistent, yet I found the hooks came up short. Although I can understand why they work so well in some other fishing styles such as offshore fishing, surf fishing conditions don't seem to be a good match. In offshore fishing the captain controls the boat so that fish can't overrun the boat. So, if a marlin or sailfish takes the bait, the boat puts constant pressure on the hook and there is no slack. However, in the surf, it is very difficult to be sure which way the fish is moving, or own certainty there is no slack in the line. Even a little slack provides a fish with the chance to spit the bait and the hook before it is in position to drag along the inside of the mouth, turn, and find the corner of the mouth. Maybe others have found a way to make this work, but I can't. Besides, since I hold the rod and set the hook quickly, the circle hook becomes superfluous.

Hooks For Worms:

I use 1/0 or 2/0 bait-saver hooks when fishing with worms. I'll discuss the rig later. You want a light hook in this style of bait fishing because the idea is for the worms to drift about as naturally as possible in the surf. A heavy hook would drag the worms to the bottom, and that isn't as good a presentation as when they gently sway in the currents a foot or so above the sand. The downside is that these hooks are weak. They snap easily and they rust easily. To solve this problem, I fish with a looser drag than I would when chunking, and I don't use rusted hooks.

Hooks For Live Eels:

Most anglers use a beaked short shank hook (often in the 5/0 size). There are two popular ways to hook the eels. The first method is to weave the hook through the nostrils, but with repeated casts the nostril holes enlarge and eels often fall off. Others suggest going in under the chin and out an eye socket. It's a better hook hold, but the eels react with more energy to this approach. Eels are slimy, so have a rag handy to get a solid grip on the eel. Live eels add a lot of energy to the presentation, but active eels twist around the line, too. To solve this problem, many anglers hold the eels by the head with a rag and smack it against the sand or a piece of wood. That breaks a few vertebrae and slows the eel down. The eel still moves around but is less likely to foul your line. Be careful, don't whack the eel so hard that you kill it or totally immobilize it.

Chunking Rigs:

I use two types of rigs. I use 60-pound bright Steelon or Seven-Strand for both styles of leaders, and I crimp the wire leader rather than heat seal it or tie it. I've never found that motionless bright multi-stranded wire was a disadvantage even when targeting stripers, and it just doesn't seem worth the risk of a bluefish pick-up on a mono leader. Anyway, I never noticed a difference in the number of stripers I caught, either way.

Keep rigs simple for maximum efficiency. (Zeno Hromin photo)

The first rig is a very standard one that works best in calmer water. It consists of a 6/0 Siwash hook, a fish-finder apparatus using a swivel (not one of those Teflon sleeves) and an eight to ten-inch length of leader. The quality of these Teflon devices was better years ago and I don't use them when chunking because of the strong hook setting and fighting pressure I put on my terminal rig. This set up allows a fish to pull on the baited hook without feeling resistance. I use short leaders in order to minimize tangles. I found that long leaders roll around more and thus more easily wind around the main line. Shorter leaders tend to stay put. Since the rig is motionless and fish aren't geniuses, the short leader becomes more of a plus than a negative. Long leaders are also harder to cast and more likely to tangle on the cast.

When the water is rough I take further precautions against tangles. So instead of a swivel fish-finder rig that I described above, I use a three-way swivel with the running line tied to one branch of the swivel, the sinker clipped to another branch, and an eight-inch wire leader with a hook on the other. I found that rigs tumble a lot more in rough water and tangles are more frequent. However, the three-way swivel allows all three branches to swivel about and the short hook leader minimizes tangles. Rough water usually has lots of suspended matter in it that greatly reduces visibility. Fish must feed differently in rough water with poor visibility. Whereas in calm water they can approach a chunk, eyeball it, smell it, and take their time, in rough water they must make a quick decision and generally take the bait solidly. In rough water I sink the hook almost immediately: I don't even drop the rod tip. Regardless of the style of rig you choose, sharpen your hooks frequently. The cartilage and bone of fish jaws as well as dragging hook points through the sand, dulls the points.

Worm Rigs:

The worm rig is designed to allow the worms to be off the bottom and to move gently as water currents and waves push back and forth. I use a fish-finder device that includes a Teflon sleeve at the top and a sinker clip on the bottom. However, since I use a lighter drag because of the brittle light hooks used in worming, I find the fish-finder rigs to be adequate. I thread the running line through the Teflon sleeve, then through a small red bead, and then tie the line to a number seven swivel on the hook leader. The red bead stops the hook leader from banging into the Teflon sleeve and perhaps getting jammed into it. The hook leader is thirty-pound test and is between 36 and 40 inches long so that the wormed hooks can drift about naturally. Again, I use 1/0 to 3/0 bait saver hooks depending upon the size of the worms. As with other types of bait fishing, I use five to eight-ounce pyramid sinkers.

Although I always hold the rod when chunking, I've found it's better to spike the rod while worming. I have a tendency to react too quickly to a hit, and hook sets are best when the fish have mouthed the worms and begin moving away. I watch the rod's tip in the spike. When it bends over I take the rod out of the spike and set the hook gently. The hook is small and thin, so it penetrates more easily than a large forged hook.

Eels Rigs:

Most anglers use a bottom rig that's very similar to the standard chunking rig except they use a long leader and a beaked hook. For those who cast and retrieve a live eel like a lure, the leader is often 36-40 inches long and made with monofilament, not wire or Steelon material. A full presentation of this later technique can be found in my book "Secrets of Surf Fishing at Night" in a Chapter written by Fred Golofaro.

Sand Spikes:

Except when worming, I only use a sand spike for unhooking fish, baiting hooks, and retying. However, even for limited use, it pays to have a good spike. For best results, sand spikes should be long, strong, and sunk deeply into the sand. I use five-foot long steel spikes with a point, and a horizontal bar welded to the shaft a foot or so above the point. The horizontal plate is pushed into the sand with your foot, faces the water line, and prevents the spike from being pulled down by a charging fish. Never put the spike in wet soft sand. The soft wet sand is not stable and it's easier for a fish to pull the spike over. Dry sand is packed and more stable.

Savy anglers hold their rods in order to feel subtle hits rather than spike it. (Zeno Hromin photo)

The spike should also be placed well above the water line in order to make use of the length of the spike and the height of the beach slope to keep the line off the water. That way there is less water drag on the line and less chance that drifting weeds will collect on your line.

I also fish with one rod at a time, although my opinion seems to be a minority one. However, if you remember that I don't fish with bait on a wing and a prayer, but rather when I have evidence of lots of negative feeding fish in the area, then using one rod makes more sense. Therefore, I'm not patiently waiting for a fish to come by and commit suicide; I'm expecting lots of action. In my world, trying to fish with two rods leads to heartbreak and chaos. In my opinion, one well-tended rod will catch more fish than two neglected ones.

Selecting Your Spots:

Bait fishing is no different from fishing with lures when it comes to structure (see Chapter 14). Bait and the fish that chase them tend to congregate along edges: edges of holes, bars, and rocks, too. Therefore, scout an area before you fish it, and do so in sunlight and at low tide. Find all the high spots and low spots. Make a map of what you see and note landmarks up on the beach. This way, at higher water, you'll be able to find spots even if the water looks different, and you may not be able to see evidence of structure.

I fish only key times in the tide, just as I do when fishing with lures, and although patience is a virtue, I will not waste the entire productive time in one spot. Rather, I shift to another nearby spot on the beach. You might not think this could be true, but one hole on a beach can be devoid of fish while another, only a few hundred yards down the beach, may be loaded with fish.

Summary:

1. Bait fishing involves the use of natural foods instead of lures.
2. I go bait fishing when I know the fish are present, but impossible to catch on lures.
3. Although some anglers prefer conventional gear, I use eleven-foot spinning tackle.
4. I prefer monofilament line when bait fishing.
5. The style and size of hooks used in bait fishing varies with the type of natural bait used.

6. Keep rigs simple for maximum efficiency.
7. Sand spikes should be long in order to grip the sand. Never place a spike at the waterline.
8. Select the spots where you intend to fish the same way, regardless of whether you will fish with natural baits or artificial lures.

Chapter 23
JOINING A SURF CLUB

Introduction:

As with most things in life, there are positives and negatives associated with our decisions and the institutions we choose to be part of. Surf fishing clubs are no different from other human institutions and choices. I believe, should an angler choose to join a surf fishing club, that the angler do so with their eyes open and a clarity about what these clubs are about, how they operate, and what to expect. Only then can the experience be rewarding. It's difficult to itemize the pros and cons in an attempt to help you make this decision, so I've decided to tell you about my own decisions in hopes that you find relevancy and answers to the question, should I join a surf fishing club?

Ready:

I had many goals related to fishing as a boy, teenager, and young adult, but for the most part those goals were kept on hold because I was seriously pursuing an education. Getting an education isn't simply about sitting at a desk in a classroom for a number of hours everyday, it's hard work that requires a commitment to the process. In other words, if a student doesn't appreciate the value and power of knowledge, there is no way for that student to be successful. Unfortunately, too often we tell our kids to get good grades when we should be asking them "what did you learn today?" My parents rarely asked me about grades, but constantly asked me about what I was learning and how much of it I actually understood. They also instilled in me a sense of the importance and life-long value of a good education. All of this is offered so that you understand why my fishing career, save for the occasional trips, was put on hold until I was about 30 years old. However, all the while my passion for fishing raged silently inside me.

It was about that time, as I finished my Ph.D. program and accepted an appointment as an Assistant Professor at N.Y.I.T. that I began to think about a major reentry into fishing. *Now*, I thought, *this was the time when I could return to fishing, especially surf fishing, in a serious way and quench my thirst for the sport.* Without school hanging over my head, I began making more and more trips: for flounder, striped bass, bluefish, blackfish, and fluke. Often my eldest son, Drew was my fishing buddy. We had some amazing trips, we learned a lot, and we had tons of fun.

It was also about that time when I began sending queries to *The Saltwater Sportsman* and *The Long Island Fisherman*. Selling an article about fishing was also a dream of mine since I was about eight years old. Back then, the little boy even sent a few articles to *Field and Stream*: one about flounder and one about white perch. Of course they were rejected, but the letter that came with the returned manuscript was kind and encouraging: something I never forgot and remembered as an editor when I reviewed articles. Had the editor of *Field and Stream* been dismissive or blunt, the little boy might have never tried again.

Anyway, Frank Woolner, Senior Editor at *The Saltwater Sportsman* and Glenn Voparil, Editor of *The Fisherman*, were enthusiastic about my adult efforts. Frank Woolner, in particular, not only accepted my articles, but he began mentoring me so that I could improve my craft. He took many hours from his busy schedule to teach me and show me how to become a more effective writer. Frank's gone now, but I have never forgotten him or his kindness and mentoring. Wherever you are, Frank, many thanks.

Glenn became a friend and an enthusiastic supporter, and I owe him a lot too because he provided me with a platform for my ideas and a regular means to improve my craft.

Fishing reemerged in my life in several ways, and another area involved thinking about joining a surf-fishing club. I sent a letter to Frank Keating, who wrote an outdoor column for *The Long Island Press*, which was at the time an important newspaper in Brooklyn, Queens, and Long Island. I inquired about the pros and cons of joining a club. He was kind and wrote back to me explaining a lot about how clubs are organized and how they work. He also suggested three clubs that he believed were top notch. I called each club, asked if I could come down and see what the meetings were about, all three graciously invited me, and I visited all of them. Ultimately, I joined The High Hill Striper Club in the 1970s, and was a member of that club for well over twenty years. Then, in 2002, seven members of High Hill split off to form a new club, The Traditional Surfcasters. We had no rift with High Hill; rather our primary goal in forming the new club was to keep the traditional aspects of surf fishing alive. I've been a member of the Traditional since it was formed in 2002.

I have experienced my membership in both clubs as very positive. I met lots of fellow anglers and still call a number of them my friends. I enjoyed, and continue to enjoy the competition, although I'm getting too old to compete seriously, and I cherish the common thread of activism to protect our marine fisheries resources that was and is alive in both clubs. As a member of High Hill I met surf fishing icons such as Jack Frech, Bob Rance, Fred Schwab, and Willy Young; just to name a few. Walking among giants was a terrific opportunity to learn, and I believe I took every opportunity to learn everything I could. My angling

Clubs promote friendship and a spirit of cooperative angling. (Zeno Hromin photo)

learning curve accelerated thanks to membership in The High Hill Club, as did the depth of my understanding of the role of anglers in the ongoing process of protecting our fisheries. That's a summary of why and how I joined a club as well as glimpse of what I got out of it.

Summary Of Pros:

Let me summarize the key points from my story that I believe are relevant to all.

1. Membership in a surf-fishing club may accelerate an angler's learning curve.
2. Belonging to an organization where members share common interests and goals.
3. Making new friends, and some of them for a lifetime.
4. Enjoying competitive surf fishing, personal accomplishments, and collective club accomplishments.
5. Learning new skills from discussions, formal presentations, and fishing together.
6. Perhaps having a mentor to guide you along the learning curve.
7. Gaining a legitimate entry into the politics and social efforts to protect the fish we love from exploitation.

What Not To Expect:

At the beginning of my story I suggested that anglers think about what they might be getting into and that, like all human organizations, there are pros and the cons. Beginning your tenure in a club with your eyes wide open will minimize the impact of the cons as well as any negative circumstances that might come up now and then. Remember that the larger the organization, the more varied will be individual points of view, and consequently, the greater the chance for misunderstandings and disagreements. When our eyes see all the colors in the rainbow rather than only the rosy ones, the impact of minor club problems becomes minimal. Here's a list of what not to expect.

"How-to's" at club meeting provide opportunities to learn new things and share different ideas. (Zeno Hromin photo)

1. Don't expect club members to open their logbooks for you.
2. Don't expect club members to draw "pirate maps" to their favorite spots.
3. Don't expect to fish and socialize with all club members equally.
4. Don't expect information if you have none to give.
5. Don't expect to like all members equally.
6. Don't expect members to be like you in thought or practice, but rather relish the differences.
7. Don't expect to become an expert "overnight." The learning curve takes time and hard work, but has its own rewards.
8. Don't expect that there will be no cliques in the club. Differences among members, just like those among people on the block where you live and the place where you work, cause people to have more or less affinity for

each other. Join a clique or, if you don't like any of them, form your own.

9. Don't expect an active voice immediately. Be respectful and sit back and observe how things work in the club before opening your mouth and voicing your individuality. That demonstrates respect for both the club and the established members who run it.

Competition:

Competition is a funny thing. It sometimes makes pros out of novices, and sometimes it makes monsters out of nice guys. Some people thrust themselves into club competition and find they are overwhelmed by it, can't adjust to it, never learn how to handle it, develop a disdain for it, and sulk off in disgust. Often, such anglers leave the club. It's important to put competition in a proper perspective. Sure, it can be motivating and can come to hold considerable significance for us, but in the light of day, inter and intra club competition is only a game, and should never be more important than other things such as family, friends, careers, and health. In its place, competition can be a lot of fun as well as an impetus for becoming a much better surf angler.

Not all club members view competition the same way. Some guys are all-in, while others prefer to compete less vigorously, and still others not at all. All approaches are valid, and there is room for all of them. What isn't valid should one choose to be less competitive, is an envy of those who are all-in and succeed regularly, or for high achievers to hold less competitive members in disdain.

Competitive sport requires an odd sort of demeanor. Oddly, we must learn how to lose before we can learn how to win. We must learn to lose graciously and without becoming disenchanted or discouraged. We must learn to turn loses and failures into motivations. Once we do that, we are ready to win. However, it's at this point that something else odd occurs. At a moment in time when an angler believes that they've honed their skills to a sharp edge, learned many lessons, and understand

Joining a club accelerates your learning curve towards becoming a better surf angler. (Zeno Hromin photo)

how to fish hard, they are surprised to discover that they don't win. The reason is they don't yet know how to win. They believe success is about skill and hard work alone and, to a large extent that view is correct. However, it isn't the entire picture. We compete against others, but we also compete against ourselves. That is, we continue to strive to improve and do not allow ourselves to be content with any given level of knowledge, skill, and accomplishment. So, as it turns out, psychology plays an important role in determining whether we win or lose.

For example, we must learn a discipline to stay within ourselves, and not be psyched out by the accomplishments of others. Competitive surf fishing is a marathon, not a sprint. Awards aren't won in a week, but in a season. During the marathon it is likely that fellow competitors will surge ahead of you, and then fall back. Each angler will have both winning and losing moments. The winning ones shouldn't make us cocky, and the losing ones should not fill us with despair. It is important not to get too high or too low, and to see the bigger season and the bigger picture. Always fish to your strengths, and not the strengths of others. Never allow the success of another angler to move you off your game and away from your strengths. Stay even-keeled and on course. Keep your head in the game and clear out the echoes of other anglers. That's how to win and sometimes learning to elevate your psyche to such a level isn't easy. Many very skilled competitors have fallen by the wayside because they refused to acknowledge the importance of psychology to the process of winning.

On more than one occasion during my prime years, I was approached by a fellow competitor who told me he was going to beat me. I wasn't intimidated, didn't quake in my boots, or stay up nights refining my strategy for the year's competition. Instead, I used the warning as motivation. The words awakened me, and gave me reasons to make a trip into the cold, stay longer, make more casts, and hone a finer edge to my competitive blade. Those anglers, all fine people and several quite skilled, hadn't yet learned how to win.

Summing Up:

Surf fishing is an amazing sport. It isn't the easiest way to fish, but it is among the more rewarding ways to fish. Just as the saying, "If you can make it in New York, you can make it anywhere," applies to the Big Apple, so too is it true that if you can make it in surf fishing, you can be successful in any type of fishing. Likewise, joining a surf fishing club can be one of the best things you'll ever do in your fishing life, but always remember that we get out of something that which we put into it.

Good luck, be a good steward of the seas, practice catch and release, and respect the sport as much as you love it!